LET'S GET THIS
STRAIGHT

The Ultimate HANDBOOK for Youth with LGBTQ PARENTS

Tina Fakhrid-Deen with **COLAGE**

SEAL PRESS

Published by
Seal Press
A Member of the Perseus Books Group
1700 Fourth Street | Berkeley, California

Library of Congress Cataloging-in-Publication Data
Fakhrid-Deen, Tina, 1973-
Let's get this straight : the ultimate handbook for youth with LGBTQ parents / by Tina Fakhrid-Deen with COLAGE.
p.   cm.
ISBN 978-1-58005-333-4
1. Children of gay parents. 2. Children of gay parents—Psychology. 3. Gay parents. 4. Parent and child. I. COLAGE. II. Title.
HQ777.8.F35 2010
306.874086'64—dc22
2010001775

Cover design by Domini Dragoone
Interior design by Kate Basart/Union Pageworks
Printed in the United States of America by Berryville Graphics
Distributed by Publishers Group West

In order to protect the identities of those people who were kind enough to share their stories to benefit the reader, some names have been changed.

Contents

Introduction

Hello! My name is Tina and my mother is a lesbian. I have partnered with
COLAGE, a national movement of children, youth, and adults with one or
more lesbian, gay, bisexual, transgender, or/and queer (LGBTQ) parents, to
bring this book to other kids of LGBTQ parents because of what I've learned
from being a part of this organization. Their mission is to build community and work toward social justice through youth empowerment, leadership development, education, and advocacy.

I first found COLAGE in 2000, when I volunteered to assist at an LGBTQ
family conference held at Oakton Community College in Des Plaines, Illinois. I was employed there and had a lesbian colleague who invited me to
help out because she knew that my mother was a lesbian. I volunteered
with COLAGE for the youth programming portion of the conference. It was
there that I saw more than three individuals with LGBTQ parents in the same
room at the same time. I was blown away at the dozen or so faces looking
into each other's lives and creating the connections that I never had growing up. That early experience helped me see that I was far from being the
only person on the planet with an LGBTQ parent, a revelation that changed

my life. In 2000, I started the Chicago chapter of COLAGE and coordinated it for eight years. Throughout my time there, I learned that although I was about fifteen years older than my attendees, we shared many of the same feelings and experiences. We had similar questions and struggles. I also realized that many of them came looking for the same thing that I once sought—a meaningful connection to others with similar families. As a high school teacher, I often come across LGBTQ teens, as well as teens with one or more LGBTQ parents. As a result of my own experiences, I am able to provide a safe space for them to talk and help them to develop a stronger sense of community at our school. I am also able to challenge the wider student community on their homophobia/transphobia and help individual teens who are dealing with the discriminatory behaviors and attitudes that some of the other students might exhibit. It is unfortunate, but I find that many of today's students are confronted with the same disdain for and ignorance about the LGBTQ community that I experienced as a teenager at school in the 1980s.

My goal is that this book will give you answers to questions you have, tools to know how to talk to people about your family, and information that will serve you and your family. As a child, I longed to reach out to others with LGBTQ parents to share secrets, to complain about my mom not being a girly girl, or to gossip about the crazy stuff I saw at Gay Pride. I didn't feel like I could do that, though, because I worried that people wouldn't understand what it was like for me. Sometimes I felt like my life was a big secret. Sometimes I resented my mother for being a lesbian. Oftentimes, I felt lonely and isolated, like no one could possibly understand my family or me.

For me, finding COLAGE was like finding a family. Being in a relationship with others who had LGBTQ parents gave me that sense of community I'd always longed for as a child. *Let's Get This Straight* is specifically designed with the idea of community in mind; its purpose is to create that sense of feeling connected to something larger than our own families and to make sense of both the wonderful and more challenging aspects of having an LGBTQ parent. We may not live next door to each other or attend the same schools, but we are present—and in large numbers.

Statistics tell us that there are about ten to fourteen million children living with LGBTQ parents in America alone. But whether there are one hundred people or more than twenty million is actually beside the point. What matters is that we *do* exist, and we deserve to be acknowledged. We also deserve to be treated with dignity and respect and not like faceless statistics to be studied or merely discussed.

There are too many "family" groups, religious leaders, and lawmakers telling us who our families are and debating about how we'll "turn out". It's impossible to predict, however, how any given person who grows up with an LGBTQ parent will turn out because each of our experiences is different. With this book, I'm proposing that it's time we start talking about our families out loud so that others won't steal our voices or make up imaginary outcomes. *Let's Get This Straight* is a stepping stone to help young people reclaim their voices, connect to each other, and share an intimate part of their lives, their families, with the world. *Let's Get This Straight* is for all of the youth in sexual-minority families battling against often "homo-hostile" environments, including schools, communities, and religious institutions. The stories you'll hear and the advice you'll get within these pages will help you reclaim those spaces and create your own when necessary. Welcome to a space where you are not the only person with a lesbian, gay, bisexual, transgender, and/or queer parent. Oftentimes we feel invisible, isolated, or disregarded. Some of you may be the only one at school or on your block with an LGBTQ parent. Others of you may have felt angry with your parent or parents at times for being so different from the parents of your friends. Times are few and far between when we are completely surrounded by others living in LGBTQ families. Therefore, we are constantly trying to figure out where and how we fit in.

If you're lucky, you've been able to meet other kids in your situation at summer camps for LGBTQ families (like Mountain Meadow, a camp for alternative families), at COLAGE events, or aboard the "R" Family vacations. As wonderful and fulfilling as these outlets can be, they are only available a few times a year in most areas, if at all. And for lots of you, those kinds of events might not be on the top of your family's priority list, or they might be inaccessible because of where you live. This book is for all of you—those who are connected to other kids of LGBTQ parents and those of you who don't know a single other person with a queer parent.

The best part about this book is that a community of individuals with LGBTQ parents created it. I didn't and couldn't have written such an important work by myself. COLAGE and I received loads of guidance and support from many intelligent, brave, and inspiring tweens, teens, and young adults with LGBTQ parents. These individuals shared their personal stories and provided solutions to complicated issues like coming out, internalized homophobia, and surviving parent break-ups.

Since these voices are critical to this book, we would like to quickly share, statistically, who these wonderful participants are. Forty-four youth and adults with one or more LGBTQ parents were interviewed, or they provided their experiences through various questionnaires. The participants ranged in age from 8 to 36. Thirty participants were between the ages of 8 and 21; fourteen were between the ages of 24 and 36. A majority of the participants (57 percent) identified as biracial, multiracial, or persons of color. Twenty-five percent of the participants identified as low-income. Eighteen percent identified as second generation, which means that they, like their parents, identify as lesbian, gay, bisexual, transgender, or queer (LGBTQ). The majority of the participants have lesbian parents, whereas we had fewer participants with gay dads and transgender parents. Regardless of their backgrounds, all of the participants poured out their hearts to share the realities—the good and the bad—of growing up in an LGBTQ household while living in a homophobic and transphobic society.

Let's Get This Straight isn't just something to read. It is a call to action. The goal of this book is to empower you to think for yourself, to fight for social justice, and to live your life on your own terms. It is the kind of book that you can pick up whenever you need it, whether it's to get more information about a serious issue or to do some private journaling about what you are feeling or experiencing.

I have worked with many youth with LGBTQ parents through my volunteerism at COLAGE in the past ten years. Some might rush to call me an expert on issues regarding youth with LGBTQ parents simply because I've written a book, but I am only an expert of my own experiences. Mostly, I am an educator. My goal is to educate and empower youth with LGBTQ parents to live their lives with pride and respect for diversity instead of in shame, secrecy, and fear. Each person with an LGBTQ parent, regardless of age or how different our views may be, is an expert on having LGBTQ parents because we are the ones living these experiences. Hear that? *You* are the expert. No one can tell your story better or more accurately than you can.

How to Get the Most Out of **This Book**

You're probably wondering what, exactly, can be found in this book. First, we start off with definitions so that you can become familiar with terms that are used throughout these pages. Chapter 1 highlights the various family structures within LGBTQ homes. You will learn about the different challenges that face certain family structures and hear from young people who either currently live or have lived in a variety of family situations that you might relate to.

Chapter 2 is about the coming-out process. This chapter provides personal stories about when and how LGBTQ parents have come out to their children. It also highlights the challenges that can surface when youth with LGBTQ parents come out to others about having gay parents.

Chapter 3 discusses the barriers that sometimes get in the way of us fully accepting our parents.

Chapters 4 and 5 explore common challenges that middle school and high school students in LGBTQ households face, such as teasing, homo-hostility, and feelings of invisibility.

Chapter 6 is about religion and the debates surrounding homosexuality. This chapter answers the question, "Is homosexuality a sin?"

Chapter 7 is concerned with activism, and focuses on teaching youth with LGBTQ parents how to make this world a better place by becoming active, concerned citizens.

GO DEEPER

Try to answer the questions in each chapter. Your answers may surprise, enlighten, or confound you. Your responses create a space for inner dialogue to occur and for you to go deeper into yourself, critically analyzing your thoughts and values. You have to understand yourself before you can expect others to understand you.

BE VULNERABLE

Sometimes it's hard to shake off that thick shell and be completely open and honest with ourselves and with others. Saying what's really on your mind can be scary or uncomfortable. It can also be liberating. Break through that barrier and show your true self, in all of its precious vulnerability and wonder. That's where total acceptance and self-understanding begins.

START JOURNALING

If you aren't already doing so, start writing down your everyday feelings and happenings. You can write in a fancy journal, an old spiral notebook, on a computer, or right here in this book (we provide you with lined pages at the end of each chapter). It is a fantastic way to get stuff out of your head and into the universe. Journaling can reduce stress and help you gain perspective. You get to release daily frustrations onto the page (or screen) and quietly celebrate your successes. Life goes by fast; write it down so that you don't forget it.

SPEAK UP

You have thoughts, feelings, opinions, and valuable life experiences that make you who you are. Remember, *you* are the expert. Don't keep your perspective on life bottled up inside. Although there may be a variety of experiences featured here that do not resemble yours, it does not mean that your experience is invalid. Share your insight and a little of your world on the pages within this book. There will be areas in most of the chapters for you to write about yourself and get comfortable telling your story. What you feel and think is valuable and extremely important, so speak up!

YOU ARE NOT THE PROBLEM

No matter how you feel about having an LGBTQ parent, try to keep in mind that in most of our cases, our parents and our families are *not* the problem. We, as individuals in LGBTQ families, are *not* the problem. Sadly though, we live in a world that can be pretty mean around LGBTQ stuff, and *that* is the real problem.

We hope that you find this book engaging and easy to use. We also hope you will be able to apply some of the tools and tips given in this book immediately and in your everyday life.

Breakin' It Down: **Definitions**

It is important that we're all on the same page, so here I'm going to take a moment to define some potentially confusing terms that are used throughout this book. Some of the terms are specific to the lesbian, gay, bisexual, transgender, and queer (LGBTQ) community or LGBTQ families; a few words will be slang terms that are used in popular culture; and the rest will be general terms or acronyms you may or may not be familiar with. The definitions used have been pulled from inside my brain and from other fabulous sources, such as the Gender Equity Resource Center website at University of California—Berkeley, COLAGE, and another ultrasmart friend: author/COLAGEr Abigail Garner. These are not the only definitions out there, but the glossary below will explain what we mean when we use certain words or terms in this book.

ally	a person or group that supports another group's beliefs and causes.
bias	dislike of a person or group, usually based on stereotypes, lack of knowledge, or a personal experience.
bisexual	a person who is attracted to men and women.
bothie	a person with two parents, one male and one female, and both parents identify as LGBTQ.
blended family	a family made up of children from different parents or partners.
butch	a person whose gender expression is more traditionally masculine.
classism	discriminated based on income level (i.e., when people use the term "ghetto" to mean bad or ignorant when all poor people aren't bad or ignorant).
COG	children of gays.
COLAGE	The national movement of children, youth, and adults with one or more lesbian, gay, bisexual, transgender, and/or queer parents. Go to www.colage.org for more information on this incredible organization.
COLAGEr	a person that has an LGBTQ parent; usually a member of COLAGE, but not necessarily.
culturally queer	a term created by Stefan Lynch, the first COLAGE director, that generally refers to heterosexual individuals who strongly identify with queer culture, usually because they grew up or are growing up with an LGBTQ parent.
discrimination	treating a person or a group unfairly, usually because of bias or privilege.
donor insemination	when a child is conceived using sperm from an anonymous or known donor .
gay	males who are attracted to males; also an umbrella term for LGBTQ individuals.
gaydar	one's supposed ability to to detect a gay person.
gender expression	refers to an individual's characteristics and behaviors, such as appearance, dress, mannerisms, speech patterns, and social interactions, that are perceived as masculine or feminine.
gender identity	refers to a person's internal, deeply felt sense of being either male, female, something other, or in between. Everyone has a gender identity.
gender queer	a person who does not abide by stereotypical gender rules and expectations but recognizes the fluidity of gender and feels comfortable on various spots along the gender spectrum.

GSA	Gay-Straight alliance, a school-based organization that advocates for LGBTQ students and their allies.
heterosexism	the belief that being "straight" is better or more favorable than being gay, and systems which treat straight people and straight families better than gay people or gay families.
heterosexual	a person attracted to members of the opposite sex.
heterosexual divorce	divorce by opposite-sex parents.
homo-hostile	a person or an environment that is unfriendly and intentionally aggressive towards someone perceived as gay.
homophobia	a fear of LGBTQ individuals that can lead to distrust, disdain, discrimination, and misunderstanding.
homosexual	a person attracted to members of the same sex.
interracial family	a family made up of family members with different racial backgrounds.
intersex	a general term used for a variety of conditions in which a person is born with a reproductive or sexual anatomy that doesn't seem to fit the typical definitions of female or male; some intersex conditions do not manifest until the onset of puberty.
lesbian	a female who is attracted to females.
LGBTQ	lesbian, gay, bisexual, transgender, and queer.
LGBTQQI	lesbian, gay, bisexual, transgender, queer, questioning, and intersex. This is probably one of the most all-encompassing terms for describing members of the sexual-minority community.
liposuction life	a life where you have to ignore important elements of who you are in order to belong to a certain group or conform to others' expectations.
ne'gay'tivity	when people say or think negative things about gays.
oppression	when a person or group is kept down by another group.
queer	any person that identifies as LGBTQQI; also may refer to someone that does not want to be narrowly defined. Often an insult in the past, many LGBTQQI people have reclaimed the term in recent times.
queerspawn	a term coined by Stefan Lynch, the first COLAGE director; generally refers to a person with one or more LGBTQQI parents. This term is now used widely amongst those with LGBTQ parents.
questioning	refers to a person who is questioning or exploring their sexual and/or gender identity.
racism	discrimination based on race and systems that treat white/light-skinned people better.

Second Generation	(also called Second Gen) a queer or questioning person who has one or more LGBTQQI parents. This term was created by Dan Cherubin, the gay son of lesbian mothers.
sexism	discrimination based on gender/sex; systems which treat one gender better.
sexual-minority family	a family headed by one or more queer parents.
sexual orientation	the focus of one's sexual interest towards members of the same or opposite sex, or both.
stereotype	a belief that all or most people in a certain group behave in a particular way (i.e., all Asian students are smart or all African-Americans can dance).
transgender	umbrella term that can be used to describe people whose gender expression is nonconforming and/or whose gender identity is different from their birth-assigned gender. For example, a person born male may feel more comfortable as a woman or vice versa. This is tricky to define because being transgender means different things to different individuals. The most sensitive approach is to ask transgender persons how they define themselves.
transphobia	discrimination against and fear of transgendered individuals.
transracial adoption	when a person is adopted by parents of a race different from their own.

A Note to **Parents**

If you're wondering whether this book is suitable for your child or children, I encourage you to page through and see what you think. It's not my place to tell you to *yes, absolutely get this for your kid,* but I will tell you that this is the book I wish I had read when I was young.

There are a few things you should know:

(1) This book is intended for individuals ages ten and up, and the content is fairly consistently at a fourth- or fifth-grade reading level.

(2) We talk about complex topics, and we are being *real* about these issues. This will invariably make some parents uncomfortable, but the goal of this book is to help kids of LGBTQ parents navigate their way in the world—and sometimes that world is hostile to the things we hold dearest. Many LGBTQ parents feel guilty that their kids experience some hardships related to having LGBTQ parents. It's not your fault. The problem isn't that we have LGBTQ parents. The problem is that homophobia and transphobia exist. By being *real,* we're giving our youth tools to deal with prejudice and oppression.

The decision is yours. Now go on and buy the book! You can always store it for future reference. We hope that your child or children enjoy the book and that it might even spark a rich dialogue in your family.

Chapter One

Our**Family**Structures

"You don't choose your family. They are God's gift to you, as you are to them."
—Desmond Tutu, South African cleric and activist

We are all part of families, no matter how they came to be. The mere fact of our parents being lesbian, gay, bisexual, transgender, and/or queer doesn't usually make our experiences growing up all that much different from people with straight parents. We eat dinner together (or not), we get grounded for dumb stuff, and we roll our eyes at the dorky look of pride on our parents' faces when we accomplish our goals. Kids of LGBTQ families come from different racial, ethnic, and religious backgrounds. We live all over the globe, from big cities to small, rural areas. Some of our parents are

CEOs of big companies, while others are schoolteachers or stay-at-home parents. Some of our parents have struggled with unemployment and others have started their own businesses.

People tend to lump all "gay" families into one big boat, assuming that we are all the same. This can't be further from the truth. Our families take form in many different ways. Some of us are raised by a single parent, two parents, or more. Many kids with LGBTQ parents are living in blended families, meaning that they're living with the kids of their parent's partner, or stepsiblings, and maybe their dad and his partner decide to have a kid together after that. Some of us came into our families by way of donor insemination or were adopted by parents of a different race. All of our family experiences are unique and valid, whether similar to those of other families or vastly different.

In this chapter, we will discuss common family structures and the joys and challenges that come with them. Know that if your family makeup or experience isn't discussed here, it is still extremely valuable, and you will be invited to share your own family experience at the end of this chapter.

TWO-PARENT HOMES

The majority of youth interviewed for this book are living in homes with two LGBTQ parents. Keith, age thirteen, used to live with his African-American mom and Italian-American father. Then his biological parents divorced. Now Keith lives with his mother and his mom's partner. He has two moms and a dad.

Will, age eighteen, was adopted by his two dads, but they separated and now one of his dads has another partner. Technically, he has three dads because he has a relationship with and is being raised by all three of them.

Natasha, age ten, lives in a blended family and has two moms and five siblings. Two of her siblings are her biological siblings and the other three siblings were born to her second mom.

Each of our families has little things that make them special. Living with two parents can be great, but it also comes with unique challenges.

I am the only person I know with a family that looks like mine. Is it normal to feel abnormal?

It's absolutely normal to feel not so normal. The reality is that there are probably many normal aspects to your life, but your family structure does go beyond the norm. Instead of viewing your family structure as a deficit, try seeing it as a bonus and something that sets you apart from the mundane. To feel less isolated, try to connect with a local LGBTQ family organization and COLAGE. If neither is available, consider starting a COLAGE chapter that will help you create community when and where you need it the most.

BLENDED FAMILIES

A blended family, or step-family, is one where two families come together. Perhaps you came home one day and inherited a new stepdad and two brothers. Or maybe you moved with your mom into the home of her partner. Just like in blended heterosexual families, LGBTQ blended families can face unique challenges. The children in the home must get used to living with each other, sharing their belongings, and compromising with new siblings or stepparents. Youth in blended families may also have to get accustomed to new personalities, new sets of rules imposed by a new stepparent, and possibly new behavior on the part of their own parent.

You may feel that your parent treats your "new" siblings better or nicer, which can sometimes happen because your parent is adjusting too and doesn't want to come off like an ogre. You may find your stepparent to be mean or irritating at first. There may be new responsibilities for you, like babysitting your "new" younger sibling or doing different chores. You are also expected to respect your stepparent, this person who you may feel you barely know, and who likely doesn't feel like a parent yet. The biggest challenge generally comes from sharing your personal space, especially if your home suddenly got crowded, or if you've been forced to move into another home. All of these adjustments can be a recipe for conflict.

Before you blow your top, let me offer you these few suggestions that may help you get by. First, have patience. Adjustment and developing good relationships take time. You have to be patient with yourself, your parent, your stepparent, and your stepsiblings. You also have to be patient with the situation. Before your patience wears thin, you need to communicate your needs and frustrations in a respectful manner. Before you can communicate effectively, you have to know exactly what is bothering you. Is it that your stepsibling touches your belongings without asking? Is it that you miss how it was before your family became blended?

Talk to your parent about your feelings. You may feel like your parent now has less time and attention for you. It's okay to tell your parent, "Hey, remember me? I'd like some quality time!" You can have a balance of doing activities that are special for you and your parent as well as ones that involve the whole family. If you're having trouble with one of your "new" family members, sometimes the best approach to solving the conflict is to talk to your parent first. Then you can address the specific family member with some support.

Finally, give others the benefit of the doubt and try to see the best in them. If you think your stepfather is evil, then you will be less likely to communicate in a positive manner, to trust him, or to respect him. Think positively, be mature, and try to understand what other family members are thinking and feeling. Put yourself in their shoes. It's not only about you.

Now, don't fret. All blended families are not wrought with drama, but if initial or occasional drama does pop up, then by reading this section you have been well prepared. Happy blending!

MORE VISIBILITY: A TRICKY CHALLENGE FOR KIDS IN TWO-PARENT HOMES

Youth living in two-parent LGBTQ homes are more visible than children in single-parent homes. For example, when your parents show up to your soccer game, most people can see that those parents are two women. Therefore, those kids often get asked a lot of questions about their families. Some questions are fine, but some are rude, inappropriate, or unfair.

Xavier, age 15, lives in California and gets questioned all of the time about his two mothers and the absence of his father. "People kept bugging me about the other woman in the car. I'd reply, 'That's my other mom.' I'm open with all of my friends about my moms. It happened after I attended

COLAGE meetings and realized there's nothing wrong with my family. I shouldn't be concealing this; it's my family." Xavier is also asked about the lack of a father figure in his home. "I would get irritated because my friends would ask me about the whereabouts of my father because I had two moms, but they'd never ask my friend who has a single mom about his father. I think they ask because of curiosity and the unusualness of having two gay parents." Being more visible is a great thing, but it can be a challenge for those with two LGBTQ parents in the home.

If you live in most parts of the United States and have two LGBTQ parents, it's likely that your family may face inequality because our country's laws do not equally protect our parents' relationships. Two gay male parents and their kids may not have access to the same health care benefits or economic tax incentives as a family with two heterosexual parents. When you have a two-parent, LGBTQ home, you're likely to feel the impact of the inequality you face more strongly. This book provides tons of resources to help you navigate these realities.

SINGLE-PARENT HOMES

The popularity of children's books such as *Heather Has Two Mommies* and *Antonio's Card* can mislead us into believing that all LGBTQ households feature two parents. Did you know that 26 percent of children under age eighteen live with a single parent? Of those children living with a single parent, 35 percent live with a divorced parent, 40 percent live with a never-married parent, 15 percent are with a separated parent, 3 percent are with a widowed parent, and 5 percent are with a parent whose spouse lives elsewhere because of business or some other reason. Being raised by a single parent can prove difficult, but many of our families are handling these challenges successfully.

SINGLE BY CHOICE

Parents who are single by choice are those parents who adopt on their own, get pregnant with the help of a friend who agrees not to be a parent figure in the child's life, or get pregnant through insemination and then raise their child or children without a partner. For example, Chris, a forty-five-year-old African-American pediatrician is an amazing single father of a two-year-old girl. He has been with his daughter since she was two days old. Chris came out at age thirty, and he always knew he wanted to be a father. Once he was ready and the opportunity presented itself, Chris decided to adopt a child.

Helena, age twenty-four, was raised in California by a single, African-American mom. They were poor and moved often while she was growing up, but her mother made sure that she always went to the best private schools available. Helena has a very close relationship with her mother and describes her as an amazing and dedicated Peace Corps hippie who encouraged her to be independent and tolerant of others. Helena's mom has been "out" since the '70s, and Helena has always known her mom as a single, lesbian mother. Her mother was single by choice, getting pregnant at age twenty-nine by a friend who had been her high school sweetheart. Given their situation, LGBTQ single parents make deliberate choices to have children instead of becoming parents "by mistake," and many go in with a strong support system from family members and friends.

INVISIBILITY: A CHALLENGE FOR KIDS IN SINGLE-PARENT HOMES

Some youth in single LGBTQ households talk about the invisibility of their status as the child of an LGBTQ parent as a positive and a negative. Not having your status immediately obvious to outsiders can certainly be a luxury sometimes. You're more likely to be shielded from housing discrimination, overtly intolerant or nosey neighbors, and teasing from other children. However, being closeted about our families is not always healthy.

Aylesha and Chris live in a single-parent family. Aylesha, age twelve, and Chris, age fifteen, are African-American children with a white, single, adoptive father. Since their father is single and there aren't any LGBTQ indicators in the home (i.e., rainbow flags, gay magazines, LGBTQ refrigerator magnets, artistic nude drawings, etc.), many of their friends and neighbors have no clue their dad is gay.

Aylesha doesn't tell the majority of her friends about having a gay father and doesn't know how she would feel if more of her friends found out. Her older brother, Chris, an avid year-round basketball player, seems to be more decisive and has thought through this potential area of conflict. Whereas Chris told a few of his elementary school friends about his gay father, he made a conscious choice not to come out to his high school friends and teammates. "I think that they may take it in a negative way or think that I am gay. I don't want them to eyeball my dad, so I don't tell them in order to avoid confrontation."

Although this layer of protection can seem like a positive, since you're essentially off the hook from having to deal with people who might not be wholly supportive—or worse, people who are downright intolerant—the downside of not disclosing your parent's sexual orientation is that it keeps your whole family closeted. We have to be careful that we don't use our parents' status as single to keep us in hiding and secrecy.

Youth with single parents also may experience some of the issues that come with parental dating. When a parent starts dating, it can be uncomfortable for everyone—the parent, the child, and the person the parent is dating. Sometimes children may want their parent all to themselves, but it's important to realize that parents want companionship too, and that children don't fulfill the same needs that adult romantic partners do for one another. If you have concerns about your parent's dating status, talk to them about it in a respectful manner. Being single can be tough at times, so hear your parent out before you throw on the guilt trip.

FAMILIES CREATED THROUGH DONOR INSEMINATION OR SURROGACY

Many children in LGBTQ families are conceived through a donor. Donor insemination, or DI, is when a child is conceived using either a known or unknown sperm donor. Sperm banks are the route most families take to acquire sperm from anonymous donors. Some of these donors opt to be identity-release donors, meaning any children conceived using their sperm can obtain their contact information when they turn eighteen. For youth whose families were created through the assistance of a donor or surrogate, one of the unique challenges is having to answer questions about how you were created. It can be uncomfortable or weird to have to talk to peers, or even to adults, about things like sperm donors or insemination.

Common issues that arise for donor-conceived youth include: questions about when they should be told they're donor-conceived, questions about whether they should have the option to know their donor, and curiosity on the part of the kids themselves about their genetic origins and whether they might have siblings (either through other families that may have used this particular donor's deposits or the donor's own family, often created years after he donated to the sperm bank). Although there are various questions that come up for donor-conceived youth, it is important to remember that each experience is different and that many people have a difference of opinion on these matters.

A QUESTION OF KNOWING

Some parents decide not to tell their children anything about their donors, and surely, there are justifiable reasons for making this choice. Most advocates for DI youth, myself included, argue that children have the right to know as much as humanly possible about their ancestry. While some parents might argue that there is no definitive "right" way to handle such a personal situation, it's important, ultimately, to keep the child's best interest in mind. The youth I interviewed were all quite knowledgeable and knew how to talk about their status as DI children. They had been told about being donor-conceived during their early or formative years. Most said that they had always known, or at least knew as far back as they could remember. The parents I've interacted with who conceived with donor sperm have always expressed interest in giving their children all the tools they can to make sense of their lives. The kids themselves talked about having these conversations and about their parents helping them understand that they were conceived very much by choice to a loving parent (or parents) who really wanted them.

Although everyone interviewed had parents who revealed early on that they were born with assistance from a donor, not all parents chose for their children to know their donors or personal information about them. Among those children who grew up without knowing anything about their donor, most professed that lack of information was not particularly problematic. However, having the option to know seemed, by and large, to be the optimal situation for most donor-conceived youth. The young people interviewed all said that having the option to know their donor is empowering because it puts them in a position of making that choice if and when they choose to.

Sacha, age seventeen, feels that "it is not vitally important" to know her donor. She shares, "It might be interesting to meet him or even just to learn about his medical history, but it is not one of my urgent desires to meet him."

Jeff, age twenty-three, does not have the option to know his donor and also feels that it is not important for him to know, but he has gone back and forth on this idea. "In a word, no [it is not important], but to answer such a question with a one-word answer would be to ignore the conflicting feelings I have had on the topic throughout my life. I do not feel as though I am missing anything in my life because I do not know my donor. At the same time, I have always wanted to put together the biological puzzle and understand what traits I have that my biological father could have passed on to me."

Jeff also focuses on the family he does have instead of what he may be missing. He feels that is important not to label youth born with donor assistance as deficient or as having a less fruitful childhood experience. These individuals also have strong families, similar to any other household—same-sex or hetero. "I have been fortunate in my life to be raised by two loving parents who have provided me with a familial environment that has been full of love and support. Knowing or not knowing my donor would not have changed this fact. I believe it is a complicated topic because I do not think children should feel as though having what I see as natural curiosity about the identity of their donor means there is in some way a deficiency in their family," says Jeff.

Aaron, age twenty-eight, feels that youth should have the option to know their donor, but does not feel his life would be any different regardless. "I guess I would say that I think it's important that people have the option of knowing about their donor—like with the identity-release programs that many sperm banks do now. For me, it's been great getting to meet my donor, but it was not something I was particularly interested in doing. I don't feel like my life is any better now that I know than it was when I didn't; it's just different."

Others feel as if their life was indeed enhanced by knowing their donors. Emily, age nineteen, says, "It is really important to have the option to know the donor. Each person is unique in their desire to meet and have a relationship with their donor. Having the option to write to mine when I was eighteen was key because it marked an end to my questions. It was a birthday that meant answers, and it was exciting. It is up to each person to decide the boundaries and extent of the relationship. Some other DI kids I know have received letters or medical and general information from their donor while he was still anonymous. Any information can be important."

Information is powerful, and it can connect the dots by providing history and context to one's life. Aaron shared how he learned about his ethnic background when he finally met his donor (although he liked the level of mystery behind not knowing). He also feels like he has a better understanding of the social constructs of race and ethnicity because he didn't have his ethnic background information early on. Aaron's brother, who has a different donor, found out that his donor passed away from hardening of the arteries. They would not have learned about this important medical information without the option of donor release. Regardless of how small the interest, it seems that many DI youth do have questions and are curious about their backgrounds and genetic makeup. It is critical that parents understand this and keep the child's needs in mind when making such an important decision that may impact their child's life, health, and future.

HOW WERE YOU CONCEIVED? ANSWERING THE HARD QUESTIONS

For many donor-conceived individuals, having to explain how your family was created can be tricky, embarrassing, or hard. Remember that you get to decide which questions you want to answer. Maraya, age twenty, who was born through DI, remembers using humor: "When I was younger, everyone always asked, 'How were you born by two mothers?' I would tell them, 'Both my parents gave birth to half of me and then the doctors sewed me up the middle.'"

Some youth born through DI have found that it is easier to answer questions with as much honesty as possible. Ruby, age twenty-four, remembers teaching her entire first-grade classroom about how sperm donation works. Others may tell pushy questioners that it's none of their business. You and your parent(s) will find the right words and the right time to talk about your conception.

DO I HAVE SIBLINGS?

Another interesting aspect of having a donor is the possibility of having half-siblings. Through the Donor Sibling Registry (DSR), individuals with LGBTQ parents have been able to tap into resources that help them gain a stronger sense of community and, for some, answers.

The DSR was created in 2000 by Ryan Kramer and his mother, Wendy Kramer, after Ryan expressed interest in learning more about his genetic origin and forging possible connections to people related to his donor. In 2008, the DSR had more than 146,000 visitors, and they currently have more than 24,000 registered members.

This organization has been instrumental in assisting youth and adults with LGBTQ parents. Many DI youth I have spoken to over the years are members of the Donor Sibling Registry. Sacha, age seventeen, learned that she had a half-brother through the registry. Although she has been in contact with her half-brother's mother, she has yet to connect with him personally due to his family's preferences. "He is a son of a heterosexual couple that had difficulty conceiving with the father's sperm and chose to keep the fact that they used a sperm donor a secret from their son. As a result of my half-sibling's family dynamics, it is not possible for me to meet him," says Sacha. Although one may not be able to connect personally with donors or siblings through the registry, it increases the chances of this happening. Also, the simple fact of knowing more information can be beneficial and rewarding, even if you never meet your donor or biological half-siblings.

Aaron shared that his younger brother found out that he had somewhere in the range of fifteen to twenty half-siblings on his donor's side. "The story goes that his donor, a Native American civil rights lawyer, went on a vision quest and was told that he needed to repopulate the earth in his own image. Being unmarried, he decided to do this by donating sperm!"

says Aaron. Clearly, one can find out interesting things about themselves and their donors on the registry. To get more information about the Donor Sibling Registry, check out their website at www.donorsiblingregistry. com. In addition, a Yahoo! group has been created by interviewee Sacha, who has lesbian moms, to build a stronger community and a safe space for DI youth. This group can be accessed at http://groups.yahoo.com/group/ donorconceivedyouth.

Not all youth find out about siblings through the donor registry or other formalized support services. Emily, age nineteen, found out about her half-sibling through her donor and has a fascinating story. "Last June, my donor told me that another young woman had contacted him. She was a student at a college twenty-five minutes from mine. I spent forty-five minutes on Facebook trying to find her. Eventually, we figured out who the other one was and from there a friendship grew. Our families have met several times. We are already doing holiday dinners and family hangouts. Our father has come to visit us twice, once during the summer for Family and Friends Weekend. Then, just recently, we received another email from him saying yet another young woman had contacted him. Now I have two half-sisters. One goes to school practically next door and the other one grew up fifteen minutes from my hometown. She is a little over a year older than me. Now it gets freaky. We both took the same guy to our senior proms, one year apart. We were both wearing blue dresses and smiling for our parents next to the same guy."

This is probably one of the coolest stories of coincidence ever. Touching (and sometimes freaky!) tales like these make the argument for knowing information about your donor even stronger. Knowledge is power and reaching out to others with similar backgrounds creates a sense of community and belonging to the wider world. DI youth are here, and it is time for us to unite and connect the dots, empowering our families and ourselves. To get more resources and find out more information about the experiences of DI youth, check out the COLAGE ART Project (www.colage.org/ programs/art/). Started in the fall of 2009 by Jeff DeGroot, the ART Project is a constituency-driven program of COLAGE that focuses on highlighting the experiences of COLAGE youth born through assisted reproductive technologies. Thus far, the ART Project has conducted a national assessment of COLAGErs born through donor insemination and released a "DI Guide" for donor-conceived youth with LGBTQ parents in spring 2010.

SURROGACY

Surrogacy is when a child is conceived with the assistance of a woman who carries the child until birth. Sometimes, the surrogate mother is a friend or relative of the parents-to-be. Other times, she is hired to act as the surrogate. Surrogacy is used when parents, for any number of health and personal reasons, cannot conceive a child or are not interested in birthing a child, but still want to raise children of their own. Surrogacy involves several possible combinations of genetic material. A surrogate is implanted with her own fertilized egg, the eventual mother's egg (when the parents involved include a woman), or a third-party donated egg. On the male side, sperm can be donated or can originate from the eventual father (when the parents involved include one or more fathers).

Similar to donor-conceived youth, some youth born with the support of a surrogate have questions about their surrogate. It is a good idea for parents to make sure that the surrogate is open to the idea of at least meeting the child when they're old enough to have the conversation about the circumstances of their conception and birth. In some cases, surrogates are family members or close to the family and so those relationships are already solid from the outset.

Kati, age nineteen, has two dads and was born via surrogacy. She agrees that children should have the right to know their surrogates, if that is their wish. "For parents considering surrogacy, I think having the option for contact is important, even if this means only after the kid turns eighteen. Every child is different and some may not want to know their surrogate. But legally shutting out any chance for a future relationship causes more problems and sets the wrong tone."

Kati's reasoning very much mirrors that of the DI youth I spoke with. There is a human desire to connect with various aspects of your culture, heritage, and biological relationships. "For children conceived through surrogacy, the desire to know your roots, to know your surrogate, is natural. It may be hard and a struggle, but you shouldn't pretend those feelings don't exist or that they are wrong to have," says Kati. Kati also points out something critical to all of our family structures—that although our families may be made up differently, we share similar feelings and experiences. "[Being born via surrogacy,] I don't think there are challenges I faced that are so different from adopted children or children with gay parents to begin with. We all have to explain our families to others, which can be hard or uncomfortable at times." All families will have their challenges and unique traits. As long as we are willing to acknowledge those challenges, work through them, and develop supports, we should come out just fine.

TRANSGENDER FAMILIES

Transgender families are increasing in numbers in America, and they're becoming more and more visible as a result. Although these families are oftentimes inherently less visible, especially for those parents who look like—and choose to pass—as heterosexual couples to the outside world, they are a critical part of the LGBTQ community.

"Transgender" is an umbrella term that can be used to describe people whose gender expression is nonconforming and/or whose gender identity is different from their birth-assigned gender. Some transgender individuals identify as homosexual or simply as queer, refusing to assign themselves a gendered label. Others transition from male to female (MTF) or from female to male (FTM), choosing to wholly identify with the gender they transitioned to.

In the *Kids of Trans (KOT) Resource Guide*, author Monica Canfield-Lenfest explains, "As you grow up, you learn about the supposedly 'correct' way for a boy/man or girl/woman to behave." Transgender individuals do not fit into the gender binary code, where a person is either masculine or feminine, male or female, based on his or her body parts. Understanding the ins and outs of gender identity can be confusing or difficult for some, even for youth with a transgender parent. In the *KOT Resource Guide,* a fourteen-year-old interviewee named Emma admits, "It's really hard to deal with sometimes.

It gets overwhelming. I remember how my life was before I found out about my father's transition, and I remember how perfect it was and how happy I was." Our culture has a very limited capacity for understanding and accepting transgender individuals, which sometimes makes it difficult for kids with transgender parents to adjust initially. Transphobia is very real, and it's a particularly difficult and insidious problem for young people.

Transphobia, although an uncommon term, is actually quite common, even in the LGBTQ community. Transphobia is when people have a strong fear, dislike, or distrust of someone who identifies as transgender. Transphobia leads to discrimination, mistreatment, ridicule, oppression, and sometimes violence toward transgender people. It has a negative impact on our families and our community as a whole.

Transphobia also makes people react negatively toward transgender parents and their families. Sometimes school officials, classmates, and neighbors do not know how to deal with transgender families, and the youth in these families suffer as a result. Sometimes children of transgender parents are even transphobic toward their own parents. This complicates matters in families, and it's therefore incredibly important for transgender families to seek out all the resources and support they can and to live in supportive communities. If you're the child of a transgender parent, make sure you can communicate with your parents about your feelings and seek support. If you don't feel like you can do that, there are resources for you in this book because your feelings and thoughts matter.

There is a fairly small group of COLAGErs (queerspawn) who are growing up with a transgender parent who transitioned before they were born or old enough to remember. Since this part of our community is, for the most part, quite young, we don't know as much about the unique experiences of these individuals just yet.

We do know a lot, however, about youth and adults who have experienced a parent's transition when they were old enough to remember. For some of these kids, it's been a struggle. Transitioning is a very personal process; therefore, the person going through it may get more self-absorbed and interested in their own needs than the needs of other family members during this delicate time. This does not mean that they don't value their children anymore or that they are trying to cause havoc. It just means that they're ready to stop hiding who they really are and that they're taking the very courageous step to show their authentic selves to the world. However, it is a process and will take time for everyone to adjust, even the person transitioning.

When transitioning, parents can seem preoccupied with their looks and things that support their new gender expression. For example, a MTF parent may begin asking her daughter about make-up application or women's fashion trends. If this is not familiar or not how the daughter is prepared to relate to her parent, it can be frustrating, confusing, or embarrassing. In the *Kids of Trans Resource Guide*, author Canfield-Lenfest interviewed youth and adults with transgender parents. Many of these individuals provided tremendous insight and sound advice for youth in trans-parented homes, and I have used some of their insights in this section. Steve, a forty-eight-year-old with an MTF parent, advises, "It's okay not to like what's happening—forced tolerance, out of duty, is not kind. Real resistance needs a voice, to allow real acceptance to come." Heed Steve's advice and give yourself permission to feel whatever you're feeling and then try to discuss those feelings with your parent(s). Regardless of transitioning, a parent's primary responsibility is still toward his or her children.

Transitioning parents may also request that the people around them begin addressing them by different terms and pronouns. For example, a FTM parent may ask that his children refer to him as "Dad" instead of "Mom." A transgender parent may also change his or her name. Noelle Howey's *Dress Codes: Of Three Girlhoods—My Mother's, My Father's, and Mine* is a memoir about Howey's experiences when her father transitioned from male to female. He changed his name from Dick to Rebecca Christine, and Howey referred to her as "Da" after the transition. This change can be awkward in the beginning. Leslie, age twenty-four when her mother transitioned, states, "My current struggle relates to how I should refer to my mother, how to introduce her/him to others, and what to tell people who knew my mother before she transitioned."

In addition to surface things like name changes, you might be expected to relate to your parent differently. Your transgender parent may engage in new hobbies and interests, and this may require you to connect in different ways. You might feel disconnected from your parent, or like you're losing the person who you've known your entire life. Doug, age twenty-nine, who has an MTF parent shares, "In the process, I somehow lost the old, reliable parent/mentor that I came to know in the course of my life." This is a common feeling. All of this change is difficult, and it's important that you keep talking through it with your supports.

Unfortunately, a common fallout for transgender parents is divorce or separation from their life partners. Although some parents are able to deal with the changes and remain together, many do not. Like any other separation, this can have a huge impact on the youth in the home. Divorce and separation are emotionally wrought, even in the best of circumstances. They can leave entire families feeling sad, angry, unsettled, and emotionally drained.

Sarah, age twenty-six, has an MTF parent who came out to her when she was sixteen. She shares how difficult it was for her mother when her parents separated after her father transitioned to a woman. "I remind myself that although my mom misses my dad, she misses someone who doesn't exist anymore. She was so unhappy trying to stay married to 'new' dad. Although she is sad to be alone, she is glad to not have to fight with him anymore. This is the hardest part for me, as I resent that my dad broke up our family and that he left my middle-aged mother alone after twenty-seven years of marriage." Seeing a parent's sadness can trigger even more anger in us. A word of advice: Deal with your own feelings, but try not to get caught in your parents' battles and/or possible hostility toward each other. You have a right to feel safe and comforted during a separation, not torn between your parents. Sometimes a family may need an intervention, like family therapy, in order to work through these issues and help everyone gain a voice in the situation.

The word "loss" comes often in conversations, books, surveys, and the COLAGE literature about youth with a transgender parent, and it is an important thing to acknowledge. Although a trans parent may still be an active part of the family, oftentimes the old person dies (for lack of a better word), and a new person emerges. This can make you feel like you are losing a parent, and as with any loss, you will need time and space to mourn. Everyone mourns differently. Some mourn by revisiting the past with journaling and mementos, while others go to counseling to discuss how to deal with loss and the "new" parent in their life.

Sarah shares her experience, saying, "Children of trans parents have to deal with the loss of the 'original' parent. For me, it's as if my dad died and there is a new person there now. I don't feel that children of gays and lesbians experience that. We both often lose our original family structures, and I have also had to deal with my dad starting to date men. So I feel that we have the extra element of mourning the old parent. It is so hard to accept that your parent isn't happy being the person that you love so much, and in a way, you have to just watch as the new parent takes the old one from you. Some other kids of trans that I have met say that their parent is the same person, just in a different looking body. That is not the case for me as my dad's personality has changed drastically since he's transitioned." Sarah brings up another important element, which is a parent's potential shift in personality. In *Dress Codes,* Howey talks about how distant her father was early in her life, when he was a man. Once he transitioned, he opened up, and as a female, she allowed Howey to know who she really was. Noelle's father seemed able to communicate and engage better as Christine than she was able to as Dick. Christine was also warmer, more expressive, and more willing to become close. In addition, because Christine expected the family to accept her for who she was, she, in turn, learned to accept Howey for who she was (even when she revealed that she was having sex as a sophomore in high school). All changes may not be the same, but many transitioning parents will change in some ways. They aren't alone. Everyday we are changing as humans, whether those changes are subtle or drastic.

It's important to find healthy (and not destructive) ways to deal with a transitioning parent and to seek the support of family members, spiritual counsel, or therapy. The figurative or literal loss of a parent is too hard to deal with on your own, even though you will probably get through it with time, patience, and the right amount of support.

We don't want transgender families to sound like all gloom and doom, but we don't want to sugarcoat it either. We live in a world that is very rigid in how it deals with gender, which is why transphobia is such a big problem. The unique struggles presented can make being in a transgender family more difficult, but it can also be more fulfilling in the long run. Leslie shares, "To see the happy, contented person she's become (even if that person is a man) just warms my heart. That kind of happiness . . . well, I hope everyone gets a chance to see that in someone they love." Actually, many of the individuals interviewed in the *Kids of Trans(KOT) Resource Guide* had positive experiences and expressed that they were proud of their parents and grateful for their families. Being a person with a transgender parent usually brings about an open-mindedness and unconditional love for humanity that influences everything you do.

Regardless of the pros or cons, many youth in transgender families have a lot of questions, and the best resource available is COLAGE's *Kids of Trans Resource Guide,* by Monica Canfield-Lenfest. It can be found on the COLAGE website (www.colage.org). Please read this guide for more in-depth information and to access additional resources to support you and your family.

ADOPTIVE PARENTS

Many LGBTQ individuals and couples are taking advantage of the opportunity to become parents by providing loving, nurturing homes to children who need them. These children become members of the family through standard adoption or via the foster care system (Note: Some kids go straight into adoption without a pit stop in foster care; these are often kids adopted internationally, and some countries prohibit LGBTQ parents from adopting). Some youth are adopted as infants, while others are old enough that a transition period will be inevitable for the family and the child alike. When same-sex couples adopt, only one parent is the legally adoptive parent due to anti-gay-marriage laws or/and discrimination towards LGBTQ couples. However, some LGBTQ parents are electing to do second-parent adoptions, allowing both parents to have *legal* rights and parentage to their child(ren). In this book alone, 18 percent of the interviewees are from adoptive families.

All of the adopted youth I talked with about their experiences spoke of feeling happy to have been adopted. They cared very little about whether their parent was gay or not. Of course, there may have been some challenges, as with any adoption, but no one reported that they wished their parents were straight. Some of the challenges that were brought up included adjusting to a new home environment, not having access to their biological family or individuals from their racial background, and realizing that their parents were "different," either because they were gay or of a race different from their own.

We know that some adoptees find extreme difficulty in not knowing their biological parents; they may feel angry, rejected, and abandoned by their biological parents. It is natural to want to know "where you came from," and it is also natural to spend years processing the issue and healing from this complex thing that you have to live with and figure out how to make peace with. In the 2009 documentary *Off and Running*, directed by Nicole Opper, Avery Klein-Cloud, a young African-American teen who was adopted by Jewish lesbians, attempts to make contact with her biological mother. She writes letters and waits months for a reply. Avery has countless questions for her biological mother that she does not feel her adoptive mothers can adequately address. She has inquiries about her cultural heritage, biological family, medical issues, and even her birth name. Meanwhile, her quest for answers places a wedge between her and her parents. It's a heart-wrenching movie, and it's difficult to watch the pain it causes Avery when her biological mother is not interested in connecting with her in the way she'd hoped. This movie illustrates a very true path for young people who reach that critical juncture in their lives of wanting to find out about their biological parents. And it can go either way. Some people find the experience very rewarding, while it's inevitably disappointing for others.

TRANSRACIAL ADOPTIONS

In my interviews, the majority of the adopted youth I talked to were part of interracial families, and therefore were among the growing demographic of families doing transracial adoptions. Transracial adoption is when the person being adopted has a racial background that is different from that of the adoptive parents. Since race has historically been a divisive issue in our country, some get uncomfortable discussing race, but LGBTQ parents are taking it further than just the "let's all get along" talk. They are putting their hearts and good intentions where their mouths are. A significant percentage of LGBTQ individuals are open and progressive enough to adopt children of different ethnic and/or racial backgrounds. Much has been written about the experiences of youth in these homes, but not enough has been said by those youth.

Will, an eighteen-year-old African-American, spent his early years in a New York group home until he was adopted by one of the white male social workers that had known and cared for him since he entered foster care at age three. His father, Tim, and co-parent, Jeff, adopted Will at age eight. They raised him together for years, even after their breakup, at which point Will went back and forth between homes. Realizing how hard that was on Will, his parents made the selfless decision to move into the same house during his formative years. For Will, having a white, gay father is a nonissue. "Regardless of whether he is gay or white or not, I love him. He took me in when I had no one. Before anyone came to the house, I would say, 'My dads are gay, if you have a problem with it, you can leave.' Most of them didn't have a problem with it."

Hope, age eighteen, also lives in an interracial family. She identifies as Hispanic and black and was adopted as a baby by her two dads, one who is Italian and one who is of Jewish and Polish/Russian descent. Hope feels like her main challenge as a child was dealing with having same-sex parents in a homophobic society. "Race was always second to the fact that I had gay parents. Having two gay dads was the primary issue because that's what society looked at first. It wasn't until I was in high school that I started to question how my racial background relates to my own identity and to who I am as a person." Every person's experience and challenges are different.

Some people have very strong negative feelings about transracial adoptions, saying that adoption by parents of another race might harm the cultural development of children, leaving them confused about their identity, unknowledgeable about their cultural ancestry, and ill-prepared to confront racial issues. Others believe that transracial adoptions can "save" children of color from a life of struggle and economic despair. Strong arguments have been made on each side of the debate, but few of these voices come from the very people living these interracial family experiences. It is imperative that society allows youth and adults from transracial homes to be allowed to share their experiences in a nonjudgmental, nonpolitical environment.

CULTURAL ISOLATION IN TRANSRACIAL FAMILIES

A common challenge in transracial families is dealing with racial identity in a society that usually sees color more than heart. We have all been "racialized" in America to an extent; we have been taught that we "belong" to certain cultural groups with whom we share ancestry and commonalities. This might be true, but it can be limiting when we speak of family. We know that love makes a family, but the reality is that we are connected to culture as well. For many, there is an innate longing to know where you came from culturally and to connect to that culture. This is especially true of minorities in America, who often feel that their cultures are less visible and less valued by the dominant culture. This dilemma can prove difficult for youth with parents of a different ethnic or racial background or heritage.

One of the reasons that it can feel difficult to be a person of color being raised by parents of a different race is that our world still has a long way to

If my parents are of a different racial or ethnic background, how can I connect to my own identity?

Explain to your parent(s) about your need to explore your racial or ethnic heritage. They probably have thought about this issue, but did not bring it up because they didn't want to make an issue out of it (if you hadn't done so). To explore your heritage, you can start with the following:

1. Reach out to friends and adult mentors with similar cultural backgrounds.
2. Check out library fiction and nonfiction books about individuals who share a similar cultural background.
3. Join a social group or online group related to your heritage.
4. Rent culturally relevant movies and documentaries.
5. Attend plays, festivals and events that relate to your cultural identity.
6. Get a subscription to a culturally-relevant magazine.

go in fighting racism. Sure, we have made important gains in the United States, including the election of our first biracial president. Despite important changes around race and prejudice, we unfortunately still live in a society where individuals of color are not always treated the same or given the same access to opportunities. As a person of color, you may experience or come to realize this, but you may have a parent who isn't as aware of these challenges because it has not been part of their cultural experience.

Parents who are raising their minority children in predominantly white areas might want to consider the impact of that kind of isolation on their child. The rationale might be that those areas are safer and/or have better school systems, but minority children sometimes pay a cultural cost by being placed in those situations. "Transracially adopted children do not have the advantage of learning about their birth culture through everyday cues and bits of knowledge, assimilated almost unconsciously over years, as in single-race families," says Jana Wolff, author of *Secret Thoughts of an Adoptive Mother*. Several of the young people I talked to discussed feelings of disappointment and frustration that their parents would isolate them in such a manner and that they had no access to other children or family members of a similar racial and cultural background.

Most of these individuals also expressed a strong interest in having same-race role models and supports in their daily lives, whether they are teachers, mentors, family members, family friends, or coaches. Chris, an African-American teen with a white adoptive father shared that culturally similar role models are limited where he lives. He cited professional basketball player Amare Stoudemire as a role model, but admitted, "I don't have many supports outside of my [white] dad. I feel like I may need some black male supports. A black teacher would be good. Yeah."

Several of these same youth reported that they didn't share these feelings with their white parents because they didn't want to hurt their feelings or make a big deal out of it. Although it's possible that your parents may be a little hurt, they will probably understand your need to reach out to individuals with racial and cultural heritages similar to your own. Saying that race does not matter is simply not true. One of the worst things you can do is ignore that race, ethnicity, and culture have a significant impact on your development. It is natural to want to explore who you are and define yourself. It becomes harder for a parent to know your needs if you don't communicate with them. If you have opinions about how you can become more well-rounded and well-adjusted, share them with your parents. They will love you regardless and want you to be the best person you are capable of being. To learn more about the experiences of adoptees, read *Outsiders Within* and watch the film *Off and Running*, which features three transracially adopted COLAGErs.

HETEROSEXUAL DIVORCE

Many of us come from heterosexual families in which one or both parents decided they wanted to date or be with same-sex partners, or in which one parent left for a same-sex relationship. When this happens and our biological parents get divorced, we have the extra element that one or both parents are also making a pretty big life change. Divorce is not easy. It means that our lives are going to change. For some it's just a little, for others it's a lot.

Kids handle divorce very differently, and how your parents choose to handle it can make a huge difference. Some parents are very mature and try to remain on respectable terms while in the middle of a divorce. Unfortunately, this isn't always the case. Parents can throw guilt trips at one another and can be filled with anger, confusion, and a sense of powerlessness. It's also common for the heterosexual parent to unleash homophobic or transphobic feelings while dealing with the pain and emotion of a divorce. Things can get sticky and out of hand when emotions are high, and it's important for youth to try to stay out of the fight. It's not uncommon to feel torn or sad or to feel like you wish things could go back to the way they were before.

In the summer 2001 "Speak Out" section of the COLAGE *Just For Us* publication, an anonymous teen spoke about her parents' divorce. "My parents divorced after twenty-three years and only stayed together one last year after my dad came out to my mother. This year it was necessary to tie up loose ends and sell the family business, etc. I never would have wanted them to stay married for our sake, because my mom and dad's happiness is much more important to me than having a 'normal' family. I would rather they be divorced and happy than together and miserable, even if it means more trouble for me." Some youth are relieved that their parents are divorced because their parents can be who they are and live more honestly.

LGBTQ PARENT BREAKUPS

For those of us whose parents have never been in heterosexual marriages or who have been with their partners for as long as we can remember, a separation is no different from a divorce. The only reason it's not a divorce is because most of our LGBTQ parents can't marry. Jamie, age eighteen, went through her parents' rough breakup. "Gay parent breakups are just as detrimental to the kids as heterosexual breakups. People don't understand that. When they leave, there is a hole in your life . . . whether that's for better or worse is up to you, but there's still emptiness. It consumes your life at first until you can overcome it and rebuild," she says. Jamie's mom and her partner broke up several times, and it was difficult each time for Jamie and her step sister (the teenage daughter of her mom's partner).

Some youth have been through more than one parental breakup. This was the case for Emily, from Massachusetts, who experienced two breakups while growing up. "My birth mom (I was born through donor insemination) broke up with her partner, who had been my other parent from the time I was born until I was four. I don't remember it very well, but I went through a phase where I misbehaved for a short time. Two years ago, my

My parents had a bad break-up. I don't want to be in the middle, but I still want to see my other parent. How should I tell the parent that I reside with and not hurt any feelings?

Don't be concerned about hurt feelings. The break-up or divorce is your parents' business, not yours. Tell both parents that they are both important in your life and that you would like to create a plan that allows you to still be raised and nurtured by both of them. It takes love to raise a child, but that loves does not have to come from under the same roof.

mom and her partner of seven years, who adopted me through second-parent adoption, broke up. We all still live together, but they are no longer partners. I dealt with it then by talking to other COLAGE youth who had gone through similar experiences. They gave me advice and helped me feel better. It is really a matter of coming to terms with it for yourself. My parents don't fight nearly as much now, which has been better for all of us. Don't forget, your parents are there to help you deal. They don't want you to be hurt and they really want to be there for you. It is the same for kids whose parents get divorced. They go through the same feelings. If you can talk to a friend whose parents divorced, they will also be able to help you through the pain of parent breakups."

Although some breakups are messier than others, you can still process the situation in a positive manner. "I did not like my mom's ex-girlfriend, but I saw how hard the breakup was for my mom. I would just say, always be there for your parents and comfort them," shares Elizabeth, age sixteen.

Many youth, with the help of their parents, have been able to keep parental divorce and breakups in perspective. "My parents' breakup was for the better and, luckily, I understood that when it happened. I was able to continue having a better relationship with both of my mothers after they split up," says Carmen Leah, age twenty-two.

If you are angry or confused, talk to your parents about your feelings. You have a right to your opinions and feelings. You also have a right to answers (although they might not be the answers you want to hear). Chelsia, the twenty-eight-year-old daughter of a bisexual parent, gives good advice when she says, "There is no correct way to deal with the separation of parents. Whatever feelings you may have about a separation are perfectly fine to experience. Feel all your emotions to any extent that you need. Talk about it for as long as you need to. Talk to both of your parents as much as you can. Take your time." Breakups can be rough, but with patience, communication, and understanding, you can get through the separation of your family.

Whether you are adopted, from a single-parent home, or living with two parents, your experience is unique. You may fit into several of these categories at different times in your life or live in a different family structure altogether. And it's all good. What I hope that you take away from this chapter is that we all have similarities and differences, and we all encounter challenges at times. It's normal and is the essence of family—some things may change, but the love is the same.

YOUR TURN

How is your family made up and who are the players? (Feel free to include parents or siblings who may not live with you.)

_____

_____

_____

_____

How do you feel that living in an LGBTQ family has affected you?

_____

_____

_____

_____

What are the challenges you face in your family?

_____

_____

_____

_____

What do you think your family should do to meet those challenges?

_____

_____

_____

_____

What is the best thing about your family?

_____

_____

_____

_____

What does your family taste, smell, sound, or feel like?
Be creative and use the first thing that comes to your mind.

_____

_____

_____

_____

What would you tell the world about your family if you could?

_____

_____

_____

_____

NOBODY'S PERFECT

Regardless of your family makeup, what matters is how you are treated and whether there is love, respect, and a sense of safety in the home. Also, let's not buy into the myth of the "perfect family." Sometimes we feel as if everyone is watching us, and there is pressure to be perfect in an imperfect world. Some of our parents try to make us "perfect" kids to make sure that no one has anything negative to say about gay parenting. Don't get caught up in that. We all do things that make us seem imperfect—and that's because we are. Know that you and your parents will make mistakes just like everybody else, and it usually has little to do with being part of an LGBTQ family.

The many youth with LGBTQ parents I've met over the years have been quite different from one another. They are theater buffs, honor roll students, and cheerleaders. They are hip-hop heads, soccer players, and video game freaks. On the outside, we're just like anyone else. Inside our families, some of our struggles might be unique to only us (we do not like having a gay parent or our parent is living with HIV or AIDS) while other struggles are perfectly mundane (we are getting crappy grades or have parents who are struggling to pay the bills). None of us has it all figured out. You can only be you, so be the best you can be and forgive yourself if you miss the mark. In being honest with yourself, your parents, and others, you're doing the work (whether you even realize it or not) of helping our LGBTQ families exist with integrity, pride, and honor.

OUR**VOICES**

<u>**ADVICE FROM YOUNG PEOPLE WITH AN LGBTQ PARENT**</u>

"Stay strong and try not to care what others think."

—KEITH, 13

"Love your parents no matter what anyone says."

—ANGELICA, 24

"If you want to tell your friends about having a gay parent and they talk about you, then they're not really good friends, and you need to find better ones."

—AYLESHA, 12

"If your parents come out when you're a little older, my advice is to give yourself time to come to terms with it. It's not always something that can be dealt with quickly. Taking time to adjust to the situation might be more beneficial in the long run and give you more time to deal with your feelings. If possible, talk to your parents/siblings/friends about it, as they may be able to offer advice or comfort."

—HANNAH, 19

"Just because your parent is changing because they are not happy with themselves doesn't mean they weren't happy being your parent. It's okay to not be happy about the change. We always love our parent, but we shouldn't force ourselves to accept something before we are ready. It's okay to miss your old parent. It's normal to feel uncomfortable around your parent when they first start dressing as the opposite gender and having body changes. Set limits that you are comfortable with in terms of what your parent should discuss with you about the change."

—SARAH, 26

"My first piece of advice is to find somebody to talk to—somebody you trust and who cares about you. There will probably be times when you'll hate your family and your life. It's better to find a way to express it without hurting other people than trying to keep it locked in a cupboard somewhere in your brain. At the same time, I hope you also realize that you're really special. Having a gay dad gives me a perspective on families that's different from most of my friends—different in a good way. Don't listen when people tell you it's a bad thing."

—WADE, 29

CUL**TURE**

by Cara Cerise, 16

My culture is LGBTQ.
My dad is gay, and he is a huge part of me.
He has raised my younger sister and me since I was four.
His courageousness and strength, I truly adore.
Some people say my feminine influence is way too low;
But my dad and my cultural experiences help me to mature and grow.
I remember our first experience at Pride.
How could I forget?
The protesters yelling, "All fags must die."
My little sister was so scared; she couldn't even open one eye.
We got through this experience clinging to my father's arm.
He always supports us and protects us from harm.
I love him with an extreme passion.
He's amazing and also has a great sense of fashion.
My Culture makes up who I have turned out to be.
I hope one day hate will be demolished and our souls will be free.

(poem from *Focus on MY Family: A Queerspawn Anthology*, created by the COLAGE Youth Leadership and Action Program)

THE**EXPERT'S**JOURNAL**PAGES**

SOURCES

U.S. Census Bureau, "America's Families and Living Arrangements: 2008," Table C-3 All Races, 2008, www.census.gov/population/socdemo/hh-fam/cps2008/tabC3-all.xls.

U.S. Census Bureau, "America's Families and Living Arrangements: 2008," Table C-3 All Races, 2008, www.census.gov/population/socdemo/hh-fam/cps2008/tabC3-all.xls.

Jana Wolff, "Raising a Child of Another Race: Deliberate Parenting Can Make a Difference," Adoptive Families, March/April Issue, Vol. 33 No. 2, 2000, www.adoptivefamilies.com/articles.php?aid=155.

Divorce issue, *Just for Us*, COLAGE, Summer 2001.

Chapter**Two**

When **Families** Come **Out**

"No matter how far in or out of the closet you are, you still have a next step."

—Author Unknown

If you have a gay parent, you are probably familiar with the terms "in the closet" and "coming out." Just in case you've never heard of them, being "in the closet" means to keep something a secret or hidden from others, while "coming out" is the process of revealing a secret to others and is usually related to sexual orientation or gender identity.

There are some of us who have always known that our parents are gay, while others may have found out very recently. Given the range of situations each of us is coming from, we all have different "coming out" experiences.

Being "in the closet," or "closeted," usually refers to people who are aware that they are attracted to the same sex and/or know that their outside gender doesn't match their identity, but for any variety of reasons, they *choose* not to disclose that information.

For kids of LGBTQ parents, being in the closet happens when you know your parent is gay but, for any number of reasons, you choose to keep that information to yourself some or all of the time.

Alissa, a thirty-year-old from Atlanta, shared, "There was fear about coming out about my mom until I got to college. I didn't know why. When I was young, it wasn't something you talked about. It was bad and everybody was against it. It was a secret society." One of the primary reasons kids stay closeted has to do with our parents' fear. Some of us fear that we won't be accepted by our peers, or that we'll somehow be penalized. For many kids, depending on where they live and their environment, the risks of coming out of the closet are quite real. Parents might fear being fired from their jobs, kicked out of the military, or even losing a custody battle.

Not all individuals are closeted due to fear of consequences. Some are closeted because they are still trying to understand how this new identity fits into their lives, while others just don't feel as if it's anyone else's business. Either way, coming out is a continuous process, and there is no single right way to do it.

HOW OUR PARENTS COME OUT TO US

Some gay, lesbian, bisexual, or transgender individuals are in the closet at first and then, as they become more comfortable with the idea of being gay, they come out, revealing to others (and oftentimes themselves) that they are homosexual. The coming out process is again quite different for everyone. Some people start by telling only their closest friends, while others might find it easier to get comfortable with the idea by first telling complete strangers before friends and family. Much of this has to do with the perceived reaction of those we're closest to. For those who already have kids from a heterosexual marriage or partnership, coming out to their own family can be a pretty intense thing to go through. So it's important to know that

> **My parent just came out and I'm totally uncomfortable. How should I handle this?**
>
> Many of us feel uncomfortable at first for a variety of reasons. Try to figure out what makes you uncomfortable and then be honest with your parent about your feelings. You need time to process. Don't beat yourself up for feely crappy about the realization that your parent has just given you some life-changing news.

involves a lot of different things: core beliefs are challenged, a lot of people find out who their real friends are, and, most important, a huge self-discovery process begins. Some of our parents come out in supportive and positive ways. Others don't do it so well.

Whether it was hard or non-eventful for you when your parent or parents came out, telling your story helps you to validate, appreciate, and respect the family you live in. It isn't often that we see families like ours in the media or in textbooks, so sometimes it can be difficult to embrace our diversity. Below are several coming-out stories from kids of LGBTQ parents, including my own. Since our stories are seldom told or shared in public, we have to start telling them ourselves—with our voices, our families, and our hearts. Let's start now.

TINA, 32 (THIS ONE'S MINE!)

"I was ten when my mother came out to me. I was living with my father at the time, and she came to pick me up for the weekend. We were on the bus, on our way to her house, when she sprang it on me. I was in shock and didn't know how to feel."

XAVIER, 15

"I just knew mom was gay because she was living with a partner. I knew officially in second grade when a girl in school told me that my mom was lesbian because she had a rainbow sticker on the back of her car."

SARAH, 26

"When I was sixteen, my dad told me he was a cross-dresser. He told me against my mother's wishes, and for a while he asked me not to tell her that he'd shared it with me. I was confused and devastated. I had no idea what it meant for me and my family. I thought it meant I was a different person with a different family. I felt like my old dad died that day. I just wanted him to stop so we could have our old family back."

ASHLEE, 12

"I was ten. I figured it out before my mom came out to me because my dad kept making fun of her. I didn't say anything to my mom at first because I was too embarrassed. Finally, I couldn't hold it in anymore; I asked my mom by writing it on a piece of paper. She started crying and told us [me and my younger brother] that it was true. It was the saddest day of my life back then. She explained to us what it meant to be gay, and she told me that she was in love with Carrie. At the time I thought it was gross. Now I see how happy my mom is and now I see how great it is to be one big, loving family. I am happy she figured it out. Even though it was hard to understand at first, I have come to realize that gay people are awesome."

CARLOS, 35

"When I was ten years old, in fifth grade, my mom had a female friend who moved in with us and this wasn't the first woman to move in with us. My brother and I used to joke about us seeing some type of affection. For the most part, they kinda hid the nature of their relationship, but it became known between my brother and me from that age on. My mom didn't officially come out to me until I was in college."

KERRY, 16

"My mom didn't even come out to herself until I was ten or eleven, and she came out to my brother and me pretty shortly after that. She and my dad were gonna get divorced. This was common knowledge, and she started telling us about how it was okay for a woman to love another woman instead of a man. I had been home-schooled and extremely sheltered until that point, so I didn't really know

what "gay" was—and I had no idea how socially stigmatized it was. Of course, mom didn't emphasize this point, so it came as quite a surprise to me when my friends all started talking about how gross gay people were. Later, they told me they weren't allowed to hang out with me anymore for fear of being influenced by my mother."

EMMA, 14

"I found out that my father was transgendered when I found him dressed in my mother's clothing."

JUNE, 36

"My mother came out to me when I was around twenty-seven or twenty-eight. Actually, she didn't tell me first. She told a girlfriend of mine, and I was really pissed off about that because I felt like I should've been the first one to know. Because I had so much difficulty coming out myself, when she told me, I was relieved, but then I was also mad at the same time. We were getting ready to have a BBQ and my girlfriend was sitting there and she was like, 'Go ahead, ask her,' and I'm like, Alright, I'm going to ask her. 'Are you gay? Lesbian?' And she looked at me and she was like, 'Yes.' Tears were coming out of my eyes because I was so happy, but then that happiness turned into anger because she hadn't been there for me when I was going through the same thing."

WADE, 29

I was about sixteen when I accidentally found gay porn on my dad's computer. I held that in for a couple years, and I was eighteen when my dad officially told me he was gay. He got a job in another country, and he asked me to visit him. I knew he was going to come out to me, and I prepared an arsenal of angry words and accusations. After a couple days, he sat me down in his living room, and said, "I'm g . . . ." He couldn't even say the word. He choked on it. There was so much pain in his voice that all my angry words just drained out the back of my throat and crawled back under the rock they came from. In my silence, he poured out his story, and we both cried. It took me a while to work through my anger and pain, but that moment opened the doors for both of us."

BRANDUIN, 15

"My father got very angry with my brother and, in the course of this argument, she told us that she was becoming a woman."

YOUR TURN

Tell your story about your parent coming out to you. Share when, how, and where it happened. Then share your feelings about it then and now.

_____

_____

_____

_____

_____

_____

_____

_____

_____

_____

_____

_____

Everyone with a parent who has have come out to them has their own special coming-out story. Some are dramatic; others are humorous. A few of us can't remember a time when we didn't know our parent was gay. More and more of us are going to be in situations where we've just always known, and that's a great step forward as far as I'm concerned. The point of this exercise is about visibility. Writing your story down and sharing your emotions around it here can help you do the same out in the world. If you're not comfortable sharing your story now, know that you don't have to. Most coming-out stories are a work in progress, and a parent coming out is just the first step on your journey of understanding and accepting your parent for who they really are. The process requires you to look more deeply into your personal beliefs and to learn what unconditional love of self and family means.

COMING OUT TO OTHERS ABOUT OUR PARENTS

When a parent comes out, we are faced with deciding who to tell and who not to tell. First, we have to come to grips with having a gay parent. Then we have to figure out when, where, and with whom we feel comfortable and safe. Telling others the truth of our situation can be scary. Some family members will be more accepting than others. Some teachers will try to pry into your business. A few boyfriends or girlfriends may be turned off by the fact that you have a gay parent. Others won't care in the least. Some friends will betray your confidence even if you tell them you don't want them to share your secret with anyone. Knowing what you're getting into is important, because you need to be able to remain resolute in who you are no matter how others react.

I know my parent is queer, but they haven't told me. How should I proceed?

There's no need to mince words. Ask them. Try to do it appropriately and respectfully. Don't ask at dinner during your grandparent's fiftieth anniversary because this may force your parent to deal with more than they want to at once. Ask privately and share what leads you to believe that your parent is queer. Wait patiently for the response and hope for honesty. Some parents wait for the "perfect time," not realizing that there isn't one. Some may lie for fear of rejection or because they haven't completely come to terms with their sexual orientation and what that means for their life. Be gentle and let them know that whatever the answer is, you love them and support them.

> **I've known that my parent is gay for some time. I still can't bring myself to tell anyone. What's that about?**
>
> Only you can know for sure. You may be scared of the reaction you'll get from others. You may think that you'll cause conflict or lose someone that you care for. Whatever the reason, you have a right to your feelings. Being afraid is okay. Being paralyzed by fear isn't okay. Talk to a caring adult about your feelings and concerns. Digging up courage and trust of others takes time.

A difficult part of coming out about our parents is that it is a continuous process of constantly deciding who to tell as you meet new friends, change schools, or move to a new area. Think of coming out as peeling an artichoke. Once you peel off the tougher outer layers, you have the delicate, thin leaves and then finally the heart. Coming out to others is a little like the artichoke in that it requires you to reveal your inner self. Sharing your parents' sexual status always opens you up to the possibility that others won't understand, or that you'll be criticized, or that people will automatically think you're gay because you have a gay parent.

Every new place that you go, no matter how old you get, you will be asked about your family. Your dance instructor might ask how you learned to move. Your answer might be, "My dad's boyfriend does a mean salsa, and he taught me everything he knows." Your daughter (years from now) might ask you why grandma divorced grandpa and why she lives with Ms. Tiffany. Innocent questions like "Is that your dad's brother?" or "Who is this other person in your graduation photo?" are always going to be there to make you confront your family situation. Giving you the tools to talk about it and feel comfortable with these conversations is one of the goals of this book.

Sometimes you are out as a family just by being together. Meredith, age thirty-two, shares, "One time we were on vacation with my mom and her partner. A waiter commented to my mother at the end of the meal, 'It's so nice that you and your sister are close enough to bring your kids on vacation together.' There we were, just having a meal as a family, and our server

WHEN FAMILIES COME OUT 61

felt the need to try and make sense of our relationships to each other." This can make being a family unnecessarily complicated. It can also make some of us feel embarrassed or feel we need to defend our status as a family.

Whether you do this sooner or later, you eventually need to come out of the closet about yourself and your family, or you're setting yourself up to live a liposuction (or lipo) life. A lipo life is one where you have to ignore important elements of who you are in order to belong to a certain group or to conform to others' expectations. For example, if you don't invite your parents to your school play because you feel embarrassed, you're letting other people's impressions determine what matters to you. These kinds of situations exactly have caused many people with gay parents to feel conflicted. The irony is that many of us waste energy and years closeting ourselves, and oftentimes friends will later tell us that they knew all along.

There are degrees of being in the closet, and none of them are right or wrong. They are just different levels of feeling safe and/or comfortable. However, the goal is to become as comfortable as possible discussing what matters most to you—*your life*. Take this quick quiz to see whether you are living in the closet.

"AM I IN THE CLOSET?"

1. How many of your friends know that you have a gay parent?

    a. Only my closest friends and my other friends with a gay parent.

    b. Absolutely no one.

    c. All of them.

2. Do any school officials (teacher, principal, school counselor) know that you have a gay parent?

    a. No, it's none of their business.

    b. Yes, I told my favorite teacher.

    c. Of course, and they've met my parent(s) at back-to-school night.

3. Do you mind if your parent and his or her partner hold hands in public?

a. Yes, I mind a lot.

b. Who cares? I hold hands with my sweetie too.

c. It depends on where we are. If we're at the supermarket, it's not okay. If we're at an LGBTQ event, that's fine.

4. Is your parent out of the closet?

a. Only with certain family and friends.

b. No. S/he is very private.

c. Yes, they even know at his/her job and at our place of worship.

5. When you meet new people and they ask about your family, what do you do?

a. I always share that I have a gay parent.

b. It depends on the situation, but having a gay parent usually comes up.

c. If I don't know them well, I won't discuss my gay parent.

Use this answer key to tally your points.

Question	a.	b.	c.
1.	2	1	3
2.	1	2	3
3.	1	3	2
4.	2	1	3
5.	3	2	1

TOTAL 5–8: IN THE CLOSET, PEEKING OUT

You are still pretty closeted. This probably means that you are uncomfortable with having an LGBTQ parent, or you maybe have strong reasons for needing to be in the closet. You might live in a homo-hostile community, or maybe you've been taught that homosexuality is wrong. You might feel as if you are the only one with a gay parent, so you keep it to yourself. However, it is hard to feel "normal" when you are living in secrecy. Living a closeted life can lead to stress, feelings of loneliness, and pressure to conform to the "norm." Most individuals who are closeted are fearful of what may happen if their secret is revealed (parent losing a job, teasing at school, etc.). Some of us would like to be out, but our parents won't allow us to. Everyone's situation is different, and each has various layers of complexity. You may want to talk to your parents about how you feel and discuss ways to feel safe while gradually asserting your family's rights to be accepted and valued (yes, that means coming out of the closet). The more support you have and the more questions you are able to ask your parents, the less scary and difficult your challenges may seem. Good luck to you and know that many youth have been or are currently in the same spot. Change takes time.

TOTAL 9–11: ONE FOOT IN, ONE FOOT OUT OF THE CLOSET

You are like the majority of individuals interviewed for this book. You are out to certain people whom you trust. Your parents are probably out on some level, which makes you feel comfortable being out in different environments. You can be private at times, but will speak out against homophobia when you feel it's necessary, or when you feel it is safe. You are fortunate enough to have a few supportive people in your life who you can talk to when times get tough. You still may get nervous about what others think of you or your family, but in the end you know it doesn't matter because you want to be yourself. Keep being yourself and keep the lines of communication open with your parent(s) and your other supports.

TOTAL 12–15: HONEY, CLOSETS ARE FOR CLOTHES

You are the future of LGBTQ families and a poster child for the multicultural society we live in. Your parent is out, about, and proud. You probably attend LGBTQ events with your parent(s) and have developed your own connections within the LGBTQ community. You are very comfortable and proud of being part of an LGBTQ family, and it is part of your identity. Stefan Lynch, the first director of COLAGE, calls this being "culturally queer." Try to be understanding of those who are still partially or fully closeted. We all have different paths and come to things at different speeds, depending on the currents in which we are swimming. Don't judge others; just be a living example of another way to be. Be sure to embrace other types of cultural diversity and

> **I'm ready to come out, but my parent isn't. What should I do?**
>
> We all come out in our own ways and in our own time. You can't force your parent to be out, but you can share with them the benefits of being out and ask them why they are resistant to it. There may be issues present that you aren't fully aware of and your parent may be trying to protect the family. Also, you wouldn't want someone divulging your personal life or secrets until you were good and ready for others to know. Give your parent that same space and respect, and hopefully, in time, they will come out on their own terms.

speak out on behalf of all injustices (discrimination based on race, class, gender, etc.), not just those that affect LGBTQ families.

ParentCorner

"Be out to your family and the community. If I can't be proud and accepting of who I am, how can I expect mainstream America to be proud and accepting of me?"

—KAREN, PARENT

We know that many of you have come out, but if you're a parent reading this who has not yet done so, please come out to your family and the community around you. Being closeted is likely to confuse your children and teach them to be shameful of your family. By remaining closeted, you are sending an unspoken message that your family is somehow abnormal and that homosexuality is wrong. I know it can be scary, and you can feel as if you may not be fully accepted in certain environments, but being out helps your children on many levels.

1) Being out eases confusion. Many parents are out in certain places, like at home and around close friends, but not in other environments, like their child's school or at work. Although many youth are savvy enough to go along with this plan, it is unfair for them to have to juggle the responsibility of

What if I don't want anyone to know about my parent(s)? Don't I have a right to privacy?

Yes, you do. You should only talk about your parent(s) once you feel comfortable. If you feel as if keeping quiet is the safest thing to do, then follow your instinct. It can protect you. If you are staying closeted for another reason (like shame, fear, embarrassment, not wanting to be different, etc.) you should talk to your parents honestly and come up with some solutions. If you still want to be shrouded in secrecy, there may be a deeper issue and you may want to seek counseling at your school or spiritual center or from a licensed therapist.

keeping up with it. It is a fact that jobs have been lost and courts cases have been fought and lost due to LGBTQ discrimination. However, there have been big advances made in the past decade or so, and the only way forward is in solidarity, with more visibility. If we can't stand up and out for our families, no one else will. Believe me.

2) Being out helps your children and others understand you as a person, not just a parent, employee, congregation member, etc. Although it may be hard for your children to believe, you had a life before they came along, and you should be able to continue living it. Being a parent is only one facet among many of who you are. Being gay is another facet—and an equally important one in terms of your overall identity and development. Covering this part of who you are doesn't allow your children and others to see and relate to the genuine you. By being out, you are also modeling that your child should unconditionally embrace who they are.

3) Being out makes you a living, breathing educational tool. Folks outside the LGBTQ community have plenty to say about gay life and LGBTQ families. They have done their research, and are loudly opinionated about capabilities, problems, and issues. As we become more visible, we're in a better position to speak out for our rights and our families. We're also helping others see LGBTQ families and individuals as human, filled with flaws, beauty, and wonder like the rest. You and your family become a teachable moment in schools as well as in other arenas. Being visible will help you become an ally in those areas that desperately need it and to help other families like ours gravitate towards the center, out of the darkness and silence of the closet.

4) Being out helps your child take pride in your family. Being deep in the closet can pose real problems for your child, as it teaches him or her to be ashamed of you and of your family. This perpetuates homophobia and heterosexism, which are even harder to combat when they are coming from within the home. Answer your children's questions and talk about the importance of self-love. On the flipside, don't beat them over the head with rallies, flags, LGBTQ politics, and gushy PDAs. Educate them and model what pride is.

Please don't allow your fear of the worst-case scenario to immobilize you and your push for equal rights. You can't win a battle if you never put up a fight, and fighting for your family's right to be accepted as an integral part of society is a no-brainer. You are role-modeling for your children how to react in difficult situations, and your actions here will speak volumes. If you feel unsafe, try your best to live in more affirming areas. Check out the policies and milieu at your child's school and your workplace. Find an affirming spiritual center. Connect with local LGBTQ parent organizations to create community for your children. You can also check out the *Tips for Coming Out* guide that COLAGE has on its website.

OUR**VOICES**

HOW DOES LOCATION IMPACT ATTITUDES AND BELIEFS TOWARD GAYS?

"New Jersey can be progressive and extremely backwards at the same time. The town I live in is pretty accepting, but the neighboring farmlands are very ignorant. My school is pretty much an even mix, so there aren't any huge problems, just whispered insults that can't really be changed."

—KERRY, 16

"It is hard in northwest Indiana because there are not a lot of gay people who are openly gay. We have a hard time finding people who are gay, and especially ones who have kids. There are so many people who do not believe that it is okay to be gay. I wish we lived in another part of the country that would accept our family as a 'normal' family. I wish that mom and moms could get married and have the same rights as hetero couples."

—ASHLEE, 12

"I live in a pretty progressive city [Portland] where I find it comfortable to be out with my girlfriend. I lived previously in a small town with my parents where it was less common to see queer folks. My parents were more closeted than I am."

—CHELSIA, 28

"Living in Salt Lake City, Utah, definitely affects people's attitudes and beliefs toward gays. I live in an extremely conservative state where a huge part of the population is Mormon. I feel like homosexuality is looked down upon here."

—CARA, 16

"Southern California is very open. I love living where there are great open attitudes toward LGBTQ communities. I can walk down the street in some parts of town and see men holding hands. It's like a warm fuzzy, because it pleases me to know that acceptance is here, just not very widespread in the rest of the country. I hope that one day the acceptance will spread. If we're such a democratic society, then why don't we act like it when it comes to civil rights?"

—SCOUT, 21

"In DC now, if you head down to Dupont Circle, you'll see the rainbow flag everywhere. But during the Bush administration, it was a lot harder."

—REILLY, 10

THE**EXPERT'S**JOURNAL**PAGES**

_____

_____

_____

_____

_____

_____

_____

_____

_____

_____

_____

_____

_____

_____

_____

_____

_____

_____

_____

_____

_____

_____

_____

_____

_____

_____

_____

_____

_____

_____

_____

_____

_____

_____

_____

_____

_____

_____

_____

_____

_____

_____

_____

_____

_____

_____

_____

_____

_____

_____

_____

_____

_____

_____

_____

_____

_____

Chapter Three

Barriers **to** Accepting **Our** Parents

"Be who you are and say what you feel, because those who
mind don't matter and those who matter don't mind."

—Dr. Seuss

While we may love our parents, there are definitely times when the relationship will be tested. Every parent–child relationship has challenges
that can cause friction or create distance. It can be something benign,
like a parent's choice to move the family to a new city, or something more
destructive, like a parent being an alcoholic. Usually, these types of life circumstances or problems have little to do with your parent's sexual orientation or gender identity. They are the dramas that every parent and child

go through regardless of class, race, gender, location, or sexual orientation. However, there are some barriers that present themselves, directly or indirectly, as a result of being in an LGBTQ family. The barriers we're going to discuss in this chapter are those that may prevent you from fully accepting your parent's sexual orientation and/or gender identity.

In order to overcome barriers with our parents, we must first be aware of what those barriers are. This chapter will explore issues of peer pressure, sexual identity, gender identity, family rejection, and dysfunction to take a closer look at some of the obstacles that may impact parent–child relationships in LGBTQ households.

FEAR OF PEER HOMOPHOBIA

Peer pressure is the pressure others put on you in their desire for you to conform and fit in. Whether or not you succumb to peer pressure usually has to do with how accepted you already feel and/or what circles you want to be a part of. Peer fear is a bit different than peer pressure, however. Peer fear is when people closet themselves because they are afraid of negative, homophobic reactions from others.

Fear makes us do a lot of things, and some choices that are made out of fear can be downright detrimental. The type of peer fear that kids of LGBTQ parents deal with is fear of not being accepted. Youth and adults alike are swayed by public opinion. We all crave the acceptance of others. It's part of the human experience. However, this need for acceptance can become unhealthy when the acceptance is conditional and is based on the homophobic views and beliefs of others. Since our peers are just as influenced by society's backward views as we are (sometimes even more so), it can be difficult to have honest conversations about our families.

Sometimes peer fear is what makes children with LGBTQ parents remain guarded and closeted about their parents. It's not because we don't love our parents; it's because we don't want the drama and possible fallout (like someone spreading your business all over the school) of sharing that information. Sometimes the fear is based on our perceptions of what others may think. "I've always known my mom was gay, but I was very closeted

A good friend of mine has an issue with me having an LGBTQ parent. Should I remain friends with her?

Sure. You and your friends will disagree on many things, but as long as you respect each other, it shouldn't become a major problem. Inform your friend that you do not want to hear negative things about your having an LGBTQ parent and that you will not tolerate anti-gay talk in your presence. If this is really a good friend, that person will respect where you are coming from and respect your wishes. Try to educate her, but know that they have a right to their opinions. If she can't respect you and your family, then it may be time to end the friendship.

with it until sixth grade, when I started to tell my really close friends. Now everyone knows and I let them think what they will. I am who I am despite who they think I may be," says Jamie, age eighteen.

Other times, we base our decisions on actual experiences we have had with our peers or their family's reactions. Jamie also told me, "One of my friend's parents is very unaccepting and has been known to make rude comments about homosexuals, but never to our faces. He even used to restrict his daughter's time at our house for fear of 'contact.'"

Kerry, from New Jersey, shares her experience of what happened when her ex-boyfriend's parent got wind of her mom being lesbian. "One boyfriend I had wasn't allowed to come over to my mom's house because of the laws in the Bible against breaking bread with sinners." These negative experiences can make us shy away from being honest about our family structures.

Although the majority of children interviewed said that they accepted their parents for who they were, several of them still kept their parent's orientation a secret from their peers. When I asked these individuals why they chose not to tell their friends, the two main reasons were privacy and fear. Many felt that it wasn't anyone else's business, which is totally legitimate. The other reason was fear of getting beat up, harassed, teased, and rejected by friends or peers. Some youth have seen how LGBTQ individuals are discriminated against and have decided that coming out about their family is too risky. These are the feelings of Will, age eighteen, from New York. When asked about coming out to his peers outside of his immediate circle of friends, he commented, "Typically, people . . . are negative about gay people. That's when the 'faggot' word comes out and they are actually saying it to hurt you and mean it in a derogatory way. I think it has to do with them being taught like that. They actually get mad about it and want to hurt you."

Will's caution with his peers may also stem from the reality that in his world, attacks on gays are real. Not only did Will get into a lot of fights when he was teased about his dad, but his father was actually beaten so badly once that he was in a coma for two weeks. It's hard to know whether that experience, which happened before Will was born, impacted the way Will chose to share or defend his own status as a child of a gay dad, but nevertheless, peer fear played a role in his interactions with some peer groups.

D-LIST TREATMENT

It's easy to say that those who make disparaging remarks about our families aren't real friends, but the truth of the matter is that it's more complicated than that. Particularly among younger groups, and especially in middle school and high school, not being friends with anyone who makes a homophobic comment is probably going to leave you very isolated. It's a hard line to walk. Sometimes the best thing you can do is simply choose not to participate, or to politely tell people that you don't think rude comments or jokes about gay people are funny.

Some incidents are less confrontational or overt, and yet any type of situation where you feel like you're being put on the defensive makes an impact. As a guest presenter at Mountain Meadow summer camp, a camp for kids in progressive and nontraditional families, I had the opportunity to coordinate a skit night with the kids. Each group performed a skit based on a true story. One group did a skit about an incident that involved a girl and her two moms in a grocery store. Let's call the girl Angel. Angel and her two moms were shopping when they came across some of Angel's friends from school, who were shopping with one of the girl's mothers. All was going well until one of her friends asked Angel who the other woman was. When Angel responded, "My other mom," her friend's mother abruptly said, "It's time to go now kids," and shooed them away from Angel and her parents. Afterwards, Angel's friends became distant toward her at school. Although her friends never said anything outwardly negative about her family, this incident is an example of the types of silent messaging that can happen. In choosing to put distance between themselves and Angel, the friends were telling Angel that something was wrong with her family.

One of the most hurtful things about people's lack of understanding and/or ignorance stems from the fact that these types of incidents occur indirectly and at unsuspecting times. It could be when we're watching the news and hear people on the screen fighting over gay marriage, or when we listen to a hot new reggae song and hear "kill a batty boy dead" (and later find out that they are talking about killing all homosexuals), or when we witness other students make crass jokes about the lesbian gym teacher.

Some of us have mastered the art of tuning out these kinds of comments, accepting avoidance as an unfortunate but normal part of life. Youth with gay parents often say, "I don't care what my friends or others think," and certainly to survive in a homo-hostile environment, this kind of attitude is one that's important to adopt. However, bigotry hurts regardless of what form it takes, and we need to have consistent check-ins with our parents or other adults to debrief, process, and receive emotional support and advice.

THE MAINSTREAM TRAP

A while back, hip-hop artist 50 Cent rapped about witnessing his mother kissing another woman in his collaborative song "Hate It or Love It." In this song, he also shared his own feelings about his mother's bisexuality. The sentiment he expressed was confusion, probably as a result of growing up with little exposure to other same-gender relationships. The mainstream trap is related to peer fear and pressure, but it falls into a slightly different category: It's about other people's desire to fit you into social and cultural boxes so that they can make sense of your situation.

Do you remember a time when you felt you were different from others? Maybe it was when you entered high school and realized that you were the shortest freshman. Maybe it was when you realized that you were the only male in your crew who loved show tunes or wanted to take dance classes. Whatever the situation, pursuing hobbies or having a family structure that falls outside of the "norm" is something that makes us pause in a moment of self-reflection. This can be disarming or liberating, depending on your perspective.

When you're a little kid, all you know about is your own family. So it's easy to assume that other families are just like yours. Once we get older and become more aware of our surroundings, however, we realize that our families are actually different. We start taking notice of popular sitcom families that typically feature a mom and dad. At some point, whether it's sooner or later, we have to come to terms with the fact that we are in the minority.

Keott, age sixteen, was adopted at age four, and his dads are Caucasian and Hispanic. He realized how different his family was in elementary school. He was an adopted African-American child in an interracial and gay-headed family. After he had a couple of run-ins with his peers, he began to lie about his family. He used to claim that his Hispanic father was his other dad's work associate. He did this to fit in. These situations become more complex and potentially harmful when we hear negative things associated with homosexuality. It can feel safer and easier to lie about our situations, but the truth is that these lies will eventually catch up with us in the form of making us feel ashamed about something that we have every right to be proud of.

It's an unfortunate truth of the culture we live in that we are continuously subjected to attacks from the mainstream—whether this is messaging about our families not being normal, laws preventing our parents from becoming legally married, or stereotyping of gays and lesbians are stereotyped by the media. Keott spoke of his outrage and frustration when the Public Broadcasting Service (PBS) buckled from mainstream pressure and stopped playing rerun episodes of *Postcards from Buster* that portrayed children with two moms. I cringe every time I see *Bring It On*, a classic pop culture teenybop movie about the life of high school cheerleaders. Although the former cheerleader in me loves it, there are multiple negative references and jokes about being gay. Unfortunately, these mainstream anti-gay representations are a common and accepted part of our culture.

Once we realize that our parents are associated with the ne"gay"tivity that mainstream culture perpetuates, it can be more challenging to be out and accepting of our families.

Most of us want to feel a sense of belonging, and we seek out others with traits similar to our own. Standing outside of the "norm" can be scary and nerve-wracking. It takes some adjustment and the understanding that being different doesn't mean worse, just different. Diversity is actually a great thing. Instead of feeling awkward, try to see being different as freeing and fabulously abnormal. Who wants to be "normal" anyway? And really, who *is* normal and what is the basis for normality? The so-called normal folks are probably in the minority by now.

"WILL I BE GAY TOO?"

One of the most controversial issues in the gay parent debate is whether LGBTQ parents will "make" or influence their children to be gay. As adolescents coming into our own sexuality, this is likely going to be a question you pose to yourself at one time or another. It is natural to question whether we will grow up to be like our parents. I questioned whether I'd have my father's mechanical skills or use drugs like my mom did at one point in her life. I don't have a mechanical bone in my body, and I learned from my mom's past drug habit rather than falling victim to it. Both of my parents are quiet and reserved. I have always been talkative and outgoing, bordering on outrageous. In terms of my own sexuality, I questioned whether I'd be a superflirt like my father or a lesbian like my mother. Neither was the case. I am my own person. Although I do have some traits of my parents— like impatience, street smarts, and a strong will—there are many traits that are wholly my own. And this is true of each and every one of us.

So, let's get back to the question. Will your gay parent "make" you gay? No. Having gay parents won't make you gay. Looking at the population at large, it's pretty clear that a lot of straight people create gay children, and we've been living with enough out gay and lesbian parents to know that plenty of LGBTQ parents have straight kids. Just like having straight parents clearly won't ensure that you are straight, having gay parents won't "make" you gay. Period.

I'm positive that LGBTQ parents consider the possibility that their own children will be gay. It's a natural question, and certainly being queer makes you contemplate the ramifications of being gay in our society. Some parents might ask themselves out of curiosity, while others see early signs in their kids. Some think about it out of fear. This last group of parents worry about whether their kids will be gay because they've had a hard time of things themselves and don't want their kids to suffer, or because they fear that some homophobic heterosexuals will blame them if their children identify as queer. Fears such as these are part of the internal homophobic baggage that our parents still carry, even if they're gay. Guess what? Regardless of whether people like it or not, some of us will turn out to be queer (or already are).

Queer kids with queer parents are sometimes called Second Generation, or "Second Gen." Some Second Genners came out before they knew their parents were gay, while others came out in their own due time after having grown up with a gay parent. No one I interviewed thought that their parents "made" them gay or influenced them to be gay. However, some did find it easier to come out because their parents understood where they were coming from, even if one or both parents initially thought it was a phase. Eighteen percent of the individuals I interviewed identify as Second Generation queers.

Jamie, age eighteen, shared, "Within the past year, I discovered that I was bisexual, but I still don't believe that a gay parent makes a gay child. My mom came from straight parents and grandparents who were disapproving. To discover your sexuality despite a disapproving environment proves

I think I may be queer. How should I proceed?

You can only be you. If you identify as queer, find support by telling your parent(s) or another adult mentor. If your parent freaks out, call them on their crap. There's no need to make a mountain out of a queer hill. There are many organizations out there to support LGBTQ teens. Reach out to one in your area.

that homosexuality is not the direct result of a homosexual influence in the family. If anything, I think my mom influenced me by always teaching me to be open-minded and accepting of myself and others. This made me more able to recognize and accept my sexuality as a teenager."

Sometimes our own sexuality can be complicated by the fact that other people are so focused on our parents' sexuality. Twenty-six-year-old Whitney advises, "Quite frankly, whether you're Second Gen queer or not, one of the most difficult parts of coming from an LGBTQ family can be separating your sexuality from your parents'. Everyone wants to assume that your preferences and choices came about as a direct response to your parents. The more you get to know yourself, the more you'll learn just how much their morals and habits in all areas of life shaped yours. Don't let anyone decide for you what that looks like. Only you can know."

Eighteen-year-old Hope's parents were very understanding when she emerged as queer, and she finds the term "queer" to be a more liberating way of describing herself. "I identify as queer because I find labels like straight, gay, and bi to be confining. I don't want to be limited about who I'm capable of loving and who I am attracted to," she explained. Not all parents are supportive of our choices, however—even when we come from a family where we have one or more gay parents. Many parents just assume their children are straight, or prefer that their children be straight so that they don't have to go through the same discrimination that many of them endured. While this is understandable, parents must be careful not to carry the same heterosexist attitudes our society dumps on us.

I've had the personal experience of being put on a pedestal by some LGBTQ parents, and this has been an uncomfortable experience every time it's happened. They tend to want to use me as the great heterosexual hope for their children—a poster child who says, "See me? My mom is gay and I turned out fine." "I turned out fine" is code for "I'm not gay." Being attracted to men doesn't make me a good role model for children growing up with an LGBTQ parent. Being committed to social justice, being kind to others, and giving back to my community makes me a good role model. It has nothing to do with my sexual identity. The same goes for all straight youth with LGBTQ parents. Reject the pressure to be a poster child. At the same time, you *can* celebrate the fact that having an LGBTQ parent might make you a different kind of youth or adult. Many of us feel, no matter how we identify sexually, that we have a broader sense of the world because we have LGBTQ parents.

Being straight doesn't make us better kids, it just makes us different from our parents, and I can guarantee that there will be many more things that make you very different from your parents that have absolutely nothing to do with your sexual orientation. But our society is incredibly preoccupied with sexual identity, so as you come into your own sexuality, this is inevitably going to be an internal process or overt conversation that you're going to have. Being Second Gen is only a problem for those who believe that being homosexual or gender nonconforming is somehow bad, undesirable, or immoral.

There is nothing wrong with being homosexual or transgender, so what's the big deal if a person with queer parents grows up to be queer? When society gets out of the mind frame of thinking that being queer is wrong, the "Are you gay too?" question will lose its urgency and we will all feel less pressure to defend our sexuality, whether queer or heterosexual. Reject being labeled, and don't feel like you have to prove your sexuality to anyone. It's a stupid debate, so don't give it any power.

THE GENDER GAP

Gender identity formation begins early in our lives. At baby showers, baby boys are given blue clothes and girls are given the standard pink getup. Boys are encouraged to play with "boys' toys," such as trucks, balls, and action figures, and to avoid "girly" things like dolls, Easy-Bake Ovens, and romance novels. Girls are supposed to be emotional and boys are supposed to suppress their feelings. It's all gender-biased trash, and having gay parents sometimes helps us break out of stereotypical gender roles that society places on us. Gender is fluid, and don't allow anyone to tell you any differently. One of the primary reasons transgender individuals are so misunderstood is that our society is so gender-conformist. Transgendered individuals are subverting the binary gender code that tells us we

have to be either male or female, and in not conforming to their supposedly assigned roles, they make a lot of people uneasy. In fact, mainstream
society is uncomfortable with many forms of "opposite gender" expression, particularly when boys are effeminate.

In 2005, during an MTV interview, hip-hop artist Kanye West publicly
lambasted the hip-hop community for its homophobia and encouraged the
hip-hop and wider community to stop discriminating against the LGBTQ
community. During the interview, Kanye shared how he had been teased
for being a "mama's boy" and called "gay" when he was a kid. Having been
raised by a single mother, Kanye felt insecure about his lack of male role
models, and the result of the teasing was that he became very discriminatory and homophobic himself. Coming to terms with this was an important
step for him personally, but it was also good for the community at large.
People like Kanye West have a lot of influence, and it's great when anyone
can promote open-mindedness and be honest about their own misgivings
and failings, and how and why they felt the way they did. Being teased for
"being gay" can be a very strong motivator for becoming intolerant of the
LGBTQ community. It takes a strong person to stand up to it and use their
own experiences to impact change.

WHICH ONE IS THE MAMA?

Sometimes children have a difficult time accepting their parents' behaviors
that may scribble outside of clear gender lines. Dr. Orson Morrison, an Afri-
can-Canadian psychologist and COLAGEr, discusses his personal challenges
and shares his research, which overlaps with this topic. Dr. Morrison wrote
his doctoral dissertation, entitled "Adult Sons of Gay Fathers: Cross-Cul-
tural Perspectives on Gender Identity and Sex Role Development," as part of
the requirements for a doctoral degree in Clinical Psychology at the Chicago
School of Professional Psychology. Dr. Morrison has lectured and presented
the findings at the American Psychological Association's Annual Conference
and hopes to eventually the publish the study in book or research paper for-
mat. In this study, Dr. Morrison interviewed ten men with gay fathers. He
told me about one male subject who felt pressure to reject his father's homosexuality because of the hypersexual black male images portrayed in society.

Boys and men, regardless of race, can have a particularly difficult time with gender identity because in a sexist, male-dominated society, exhibiting stereotypically feminine traits is often associated with being weak, undesirable, and "gay." This underlying homophobia adds to some young men's inability to break away from the gender binary. During our interview, Dr. Morrison also shared his experiences with his own gay father and his thoughts about gender. Early on, he struggled with his father and his father's atypical mannerisms because they didn't align with the sensationalized model of the hypermasculine heterosexual male.

"As I grew older, I realized that what he had given me was different, but equally as important. I became a more multifaceted man and not the stereotypical narrowly defined image of a man. Most men are pressured to lose that sensitive, emotional, creative side. It is not valued in hetero male culture. As a result of growing up in my family, I was able to keep those things and be a more multifaceted man."

A growing number of youth with LGBTQ parents seem very self-aware and evolved in this area. They walk with confidence and do not fall glibly unaware into stock characters of the hypermasculine or hyperfeminine. I think that those youth who allow their parents to be who they are giving themselves permission to break gender rules and have a more holistic human experience. However, this can be difficult when there are societal and cultural pressures to "choose" your gender and reject the idea of multiple identities.

I too was challenged early on by my mother's genderqueer nature. My mother has worked in the male-dominated field of construction for most of her career. She feels more comfortable in men's clothing, and I have never seen her wear makeup. She has a deep, sultry voice, and it's not uncommon for people to mistake her for a man. When I was younger, I wanted her to conform, to be more feminine and wear bras and skirts for a change. However, I had to learn to accept her for who she was, and over time I came to understand that gender is not as simplistic and confined as I thought it was. My mother will tell you that she is "all woman" and that she is not trying to be a man. She simply has diverse interests and refuses to be told by society who she should be and what she should enjoy.

Another gender issue that comes up with parents of the same sex has to do with people still wanting to assign gender roles. Some youth in two-parent households get asked which parent is the "mom" and which is the "dad." The very nature of this question forces us to assign strict, heterosexual roles to our parents. This is an unfair question because there are not two opposing sides to gender. Most people, whether straight or gay or somewhere in between, have qualities and interests that span the gender spectrum. Don't allow others to define your family. Consider using questions like these as an opportunity to educate others about the limitations of gender stereotypes and the ways that your family defies those stereotypes. For example, one of your dads may be more nurturing and do most of the cooking, but it does not necessarily make him the "mom." Tell your peers that men are capable of being very nurturing and taking on domestic duties.

LGBTQ parents can be great examples of gender liberation, especially when they teach their children to be themselves, even when it goes against the grain. Many COLAGErs share amusing stories of being among the few kids who weren't allowed Barbies by their lesbian mothers or whose gay dads encouraged the boys in their family to wear pink. If and when we feel embarrassed or frustrated by our parent's gender nonconformity, however, we should discuss it with them to get to the root of the issue. We may also need to revisit our own beliefs about male/female roles, dynamics, and behaviors. Doing so, we may find that we can learn more from and become closer with our parents when we accept them for who they are on the inside and outside—whether they are butch, trans, femme, flamin', or genderqueer—because they don't fit into any strict box.

FAMILY REJECTION

We all have families of origin, but we also have families that we create. Family members can be the backbone of our existence, but they can also be the very people who bring us down. I have heard lots of stories from kids with LGBTQ parents about how certain family members had a difficult time accepting them. Amy, age seventeen from Staten Island, spoke about her heterosexual dad's side of the family and how uncomfortable they were

One of my family members talks badly about my LGBTQ parent. Should I tell my parent?

Yes. If you do not feel comfortable telling that family member to cease fire, then put that loaded gun in your parent's lap. Although it's admirable, you should not try to protect your parent(s) by withholding this information. They have probably heard worse. Let them know what's going on so that they can handle it, and inform the other person to leave you out of it.

with her and her sisters as a result of her mother coming out as a lesbian. "They say inappropriate things or suggest things about us. Some of them don't like leaving my cousins in a room alone with us. I didn't understand why they did this when I was little, and I used to get insulted. I don't care anymore. If they want to do that, it is their choice, and I like to know that I am more mature than them."

In some families, you can be a role model for other relatives. By seeing that you are proud of your parent(s) and that you support them for being themselves, you can often pave the way to acceptance from grandparents, aunts, cousins, and others.

In an ideal world, most of us would have worked out all of our family dynamics and would have fulfilling, supportive relationships with our parents, siblings, and extended family members. The reality, however, is that most of us have to deal with the fact that some family members will always have their issues and be resistant to your parent(s) sexual orientation and "lifestyle." (I put "lifestyle" in quotation marks here because there are a lot of anti-gay sentiments out there that specifically mention not approving of the gay "lifestyle," but as kids of LGBTQ parents, I encourage us all to ask what, exactly, that means Being LGBTQ is not a "lifestyle"; it's an important aspect of a person's life.) The people in our families who aren't wholly on board may range from a self-righteous aunt who refuses to acknowledge your parent's partner, a homophobic grandparent who has disowned your dad, or an uncle who tells offensive gay jokes at every family reunion.

Elizabeth, age sixteen and from Illinois, shared her experiences with family rejection. In Elizabeth's case, it was a variety of family members, from her maternal grandparents to her heterosexual father's family. "When my mom first told my grandparents that she was gay, they banned her from the family, and my grandpa did not talk to her for years. The point when they all started to talk and get together was about three years before my grandpa died. I really do not talk to my dad's family anymore, and most of my mom's family has passed away."

Family rejection can lead to unfortunate gaps in the family structure. However, these gaps can be filled if family members commit to unconditional acceptance and love.

In many cases, children of gays get dragged into the mix when there is drama between other family members and their parents. During my interview with a blended family of nine (two moms, six children, and the grandfather), I quickly became aware that one of the grandmothers disapproved of the parents' relationship. The children mentioned a few times that grandma had made her disapproval clear to them. In this case, the parents tried to have civil conversations about the conflict, but were resigned to believe that the grandmother has "issues" that she may or may not be able to get over. Unfortunately, the children feel uncomfortable around their grandmother, and as a result of her negative talk, they seldom visit her.

I'm happy to report that the majority of the kids I interviewed had not experienced much negative feedback from other family members. The few who did experience interfamilial conflict regarding their parent's sexuality talked with their parents about it. In addition, those parents spoke with the offenders and tried to deal with the situation.

One of the tensest situations I hear about on a regular basis is the conflict between exes when one is heterosexual and the other is LGBTQ. In some cases, the hetero parent engages in a custody battle that uses the homosexual parent's sexual identity as the main reason that he or she should not have custody. We know that many state laws openly support this kind of bigotry, and that some laws discrimimate against LGBTQ families. Another terrible thing that some heterosexual parents do is express frustration to their children about the other parent's sexuality. This is never appropriate. If you find yourself in this situation, you might not be able to talk to either parent about it. Know that there are places, in communities like COLAGE, where you can talk to someone about your feelings.

Ashlee, age twelve, witnessed her father making fun of and taunting her mother (while they were still married) when he found out she was gay. "My mom was miserable because my dad was mean and she knew she was gay, but she felt bad leaving him because of us, the children." These situations can be brutal, and if parents aren't careful, the children will end up enduring the ramifications of that lack of support. They are also likely be resentful of the parent who is being the aggressor.

My own father often spoke negatively about my mother after she came out. At first, I hated my mother for seeming so different and wayward. Then, after I realized that my mother was still a good person, I felt deceived, and I began to resent my father. I was angry at him for making me spend years disrespecting and distancing myself from this woman who loved me like no one else. Now I am at a place of peace, loving both of them, but it took time and honest conversations with them both to work through my bitterness and confusion. They still don't get along, but I've realized that their relationship has nothing to do with me. It's their baggage and they can keep it—and keep *me* out of it.

Family members must be conscious of the impact they have on children of gays when they speak negatively about homosexuals. They either taint our views of the LGBTQ community, cause us to be wary of the heterosexual community, or make us feel defensive—and rightfully so!—of our own families. When anyone in your family sends negative or inappropriate messages, tell your parents, and allow them to handle the situation. Family members should not use us as pawns in the gay debate. They need to handle their opinions and disagreements like responsible adults. It is not our responsibility to fight family battles or to be the spokesperson for the gay parent. This is our parents' task, you can leave it up to them to protect you from the rhetoric of homo-hostile family members.

WHEN THE BOUGH BREAKS: BAD PARENTING

You know the nursery rhyme "Rock-a-Bye Baby." The words speak to the Native American practice of rocking babies to sleep in cradles that hung from tree branches. The last lines go, "When the bough breaks, the cradle will fall, and down will come baby, cradle and all," and this has left us with an indelible image of babies falling and being injured as a result of this practice.

I use this song as a metaphor for this next, difficult topic. There are topics in any family guarded with a big DO NOT ENTER sign. These are the darker sides—family secrets, ways that certain family members mistreat each other, things we know that we know not to tell outsiders. Some of these are sort of benign and just more embarrassing, while others are actually horrible situations that we may long to escape from. It's hard to find a safe space to talk about sensitive topics, especially when they involve a parent that already gets demonized for his or her sexuality.

But here, in this safe space, we want to have an open conversation about what happens when the bough breaks in our families and we aren't kept safe.

As kids of LGBTQ parents, we have a dilemma that is somewhat unique. If we talk about the problems our families face, others tend to blame these problems on the fact that our parents are LGBTQ—although I guarantee that any type of problem you experience occurs in other families as well. And because these problems manifest in all types of families, we are not immune to violence, depression, and substance use or abuse. As hard as it is to talk about, LGBTQ families are not without problems or severe challenges. Some gay parents are bad parents or have made very bad choices. If you're living under the impression that there are certain things you just don't talk about, consider the possibility that there may be a safe space for you to talk to someone. It can be extremely traumatic to be told that you might risk losing your parent, and it can be difficult to know what to do when you're still young and don't have a firm sense of yourself in the world at large. I encourage you to email COLAGE, however, or email me directly, if you're in a situation where you just need to share what's going on with you, and/or if you need support or need to gain access to resources.

Some parents make terrible choices that harm us. Some parents struggle with personal demons, such as alcoholism, promiscuity, depression, mental illness, and abuse. These types of personal problems do negatively impact their ability to parent effectively. Chelsia, an adult with an abusive parent, candidly reflects on her experiences growing up. Her parents got together when she was two years old and remained together for about fifteen years. During that time, Chelsia learned that her parents were addicted to drugs, and that her abusive parent suffered from mental illness. Chelsia noticed early on that her mom, Laurie, had anger issues. These angry moments ended in abusive episodes that were directed toward Chelsia's biological mother, Cindy. Chelsia was unsure if the domestic violence was a result of Laurie's mental illness or her parents' addictions. One day, Chelsia confronted her parents about their drug abuse after accidentally walking in on them doing cocaine. She told her parents, "I watched a movie today at school and you guys do drugs." Her moms responded by having an explicit "drug talk" with her. For Chelsia, her parents' drug use did not deter her from doing drugs. Instead, her experience in the home made her experiment on her own as a teen.

Chelsia was impacted in many ways by her experiences. "I was a risk-taker. I've been very experimental . . . I've lived beyond my years." Growing up in a dysfunctional household can make us mature much more quickly than other children or completely stunt our growth. Both extremes are harmful to our development. As a matter of fact, without counseling or other strong forms of support, we may end up like our parents. Chelsia admits, "Instead of breaking the cycle, I worry I'll continue it."

In addition to carrying on the cycle, many of us who grow up in dysfunctional households carry anger, resentment, and feelings of despair. Daryl, whose name has been changed, recalls feeling abandoned by his lesbian mother. Although thirty-three and far away from his hometown of Chicago, he still struggles to let go of a turbulent past. "My mother struggled with drug abuse for the early part of my life. It was so bad that she couldn't keep a steady job or an apartment. As a result, I was forced to live with extended family members. When I did live with her, she was emotionally unavailable, and I felt like I was on my own. When I finally left for college, campus became a safe haven. I never wanted to see my mother again because of all the hurt and emotional trauma she caused me. I have real abandonment issues which creep up on me in my other relationships."

Some people living with dysfunctional parents feel confusion, helplessness, embarrassment, and estrangement toward their parents and the world. Daryl shared, "I often felt like no one even cared, even though they saw bits and pieces of what I was going through. Eventually, I became as emotionally unavailable as my mother. When people finally tried to help me, it was too late. I didn't want to be bothered." Some of us need additional support and counseling to cope with these issues. However, we have to be willing to admit that there are problems in our homes. Burying it doesn't make the pain go away.

Although we may have issues with our parents, sometimes our natural inclination is still to try to protect them and empathize with their issues. "I was very defensive of my family due to the anti-gay environment," said Chelsia. She knew that her parents were dealing with many issues, such as homo-hostility, bouts of poverty, anti-gay legislation, home vandalism, and feeling marginalized. In hindsight, she also realizes that her parents' drug use was an ineffective coping mechanism that exacerbated their problems. As a result, she doesn't consider them terrible parents. "They were very young when I was growing up," she explained. "I think they are loving, compassionate, caring women who had problems that got out of hand." Daryl said something similar: "I am now pretty close to my mother. She has kicked her addiction and has been clean for at least seventeen years. I am proud of her and realize that she's human. That means that she makes mistakes, just like I do. I just hope to be a better parent than she was early on in my life." Not all kids who suffer under difficult circumstances with their parents will get to this point of clarity and acceptance. Healing takes time and effort.

If you are experiencing abuse or the negative effects of a bad parent, reach out for help before your parent brings you down. "Community is vital for survival," advises Chelsia. Most of us do not want to be taken from our parents, but if your parent can't raise and protect you from harm, you might need to consider living somewhere else—at least until your parent is rehabilitated. You deserve to be loved and cared for, so tell a supportive adult or school counselor if you know that your parent isn't capable of doing the things that a good parent does. Please be sure to take a look at the resource section at the back of this book to find organizations that may be able to support you in your home situation.

While many of us may believe that we don't personally know any families like these, they do exist, and ignoring this fact won't solve the issue. Also, ignoring it doesn't make our LGBTQ family movement any stronger. It actually makes us weaker, because we have to pretend to be something that we are not—perfect. We must resist the temptation to closet our problems. Chelsia states it eloquently when she says, "We're double-closeted. If we can't be accepted just for our family, then we certainly can't be accepted as a family that has problems. How are we supposed to meet and remedy those problems if we cannot be transparent about them existing in our communities?"

The LGBTQ community needs to be more aware and more inclusive of all kind of families and family situations. Some youth and adults who are struggling with their relationships with their parents may not feel as if LGBTQ organizations fully support them. Sarah, age twenty-six, admits, "My dad has not been a very good dad since starting his transition, but it's not because he's transgender that he's not a good dad. Transgender people can be very good parents, and so I always try to temper my remarks in public. It makes it hard to participate in very pro-LGBTQ parent groups because I feel like the emphasis is always: 'Aren't LGBTQ parents *awesome*!?' Well, mine isn't. But just as not all straight people are good parents, we can't expect all LGBTQs to be good parents. My dad is simply human." LGBTQ families are not perfect, and we have to support each other and remember to access the physical, psychological, emotional, and spiritual supports necessary to catch us when the bough breaks.

HARD WORK PAYS OFF

Regardless of the type of barriers we face, most of them can be overcome. Every LGBTQ family will have their own unique set of challenges, but it should not deter them from growing closer to each other in understanding, respect, and love. LGBTQ families have to keep the lines of communication open, and parents have to be ready to let down their defenses in order to have an honest exchange with their children. Children with LGBTQ parents must also recognize their own insecurities and prejudices, understanding that these things can adversely affect their family interactions. Changes in attitude take time and a conscious effort. Eventually, mountainous barriers will become small road bumps, allowing you to have a more fruitful, authentic relationship with your parent.

YOUR TURN

What are/were the barriers (if any) that make you uncomfortable with having a gay parent? How did you overcome the barrier? If you haven't yet, how do you plan to overcome this challenge in the future?

_____

_____

_____

_____

_____

_____

_____

_____

_____

_____

_____

_____

OUR**VOICES**

<u>**WHAT ADVICE DO YOU HAVE FOR LGBTQ PARENTS?**</u>

"Talk about it [being gay]. My dad didn't really discuss it."

—WILL, 18

"Be sensitive to the feelings or sentiments about homophobia in your community and how that environment can impact the children. Take a more active role to surround yourself with other adults who are more accepting of different family structures. In school, understand what message is being given about LGBTQ individuals and their families. Also, understand the normal developmental stages all teens and adolescents go through."

—ORSON, 32

"See the transition as not being about the [transgender parent] going through change, but the whole family going through change. Everyone needs support."

—STEVE, 48

"I would advise the parents to be open themselves, which must happen before a child can be open about their parent. Being comfortable with yourself makes the child more comfortable."

—EMILY, 16

"Don't hold on to secrets. Prepare yourself and your child for discrimination before it happens. Talk to your child's teachers before they have to deal with potentially uncomfortable situations like Mother's Day/Father's Day."

—LAUREL, 28

"The most obvious advice is love your kids. I think it's also great if you have a lot of positive role models that can model different kinds of gender and sexual identities for your children. I've felt like I had to spend a lot of time searching for a way to be a heterosexual man that I felt fit with the progressive, inclusive, non-violent, and egalitarian ethics that I was raised with. It would have been so nice if I'd had a head start on that because I'd had some strong role models on which to base myself."

—AARON, 28

"To understand that your struggles and the ways in which you overcame your struggles were yours and only yours. While there are many parallels that could be made between past discriminations and today's, the ways in which we (your children) understand, confront, and learn from those struggles will be our own ways. At times, they will seem frustrating, misguided, and perhaps not relevant to you, but rest assured, we will deal with every challenge with the same integrity, thoughtfulness, and wholeheartedness as you did."

—CAMILO, 30

BE**PROUD**

by Marina Gatto, 15

Walk down the street
Hand in hand
Don't listen to comments
Ignore their stares
Be proud!
I will be there
Next to you all the way
Smiling and joking
Beaming and overjoyed
I will be proud
Follow me down the path of ignorance
To the road of diversity
Others will be there
And they will be proud
Always, we will stand strong
Our love for each other cannot be shaken
Our family ties are those embedded in trust,
And set on fire by loyalty
We are a family
No matter what they say
And I could not be more proud

This poem was first published in *Focus on MY Family: A Queerspawn Anthology,* created by the COLAGE Youth Leadership and Action Program.

Chapter **Four**

Welcome **to** the **Teasing** Zone

"School was the biggest problem for me growing up."
—Will, 18

School can be an amazing place where you learn about the world, challenge yourself, develop your passions, and strengthen your weaknesses. Unarguably, many school systems have become more aware and proactive about issues of discrimination. New policies and heightened awareness exist that allow youth with LGBTQ parents to feel more comfortable. Students like Xavier, fifteen, who's perfectly comfortable talking about his two moms, are increasingly common. He has never had any confrontations at his school in the Bay Area. When I interviewed him, he stated that he hasn't had any problems because "the kids are more liberal in California."

The Bay Area community is not the only actively LGBTQ-supportive community. Many cities, institutions, and organizations are getting involved with the movement. We now have gay–straight alliances (GSAs) and LGBTQ organizations in one out of every ten schools, and anti-bias school policies are becoming more standardized to protect LGBTQ students and youth from sexual-minority families.

TEASING AT SCHOOL

Despite the strides toward inclusion within our nation's schools, for some students with LGBTQ parents, school can still be a trying place, filled with unexpected challenges. This is because homophobia still, unfortunately, runs rampant. Period. Students in same-sex households often report feeling unsafe and isolated as a result of having an LGBTQ parent. In 2008, GLSEN (Gay, Lesbian, and Straight Education Network), in partnership with COLAGE and the Family Equality Council, produced *Involved, Invisible, Ignored: The Experiences of Lesbian, Gay, Bisexual and Transgender Parents and Their Children in Our Nation's K-12 Schools,* a report that surveyed 154 secondary school students, ages 13 to 20, with one or more LGBTQ parents and 588 LGBTQ parents. Here are some of their findings:

Teasing and exclusion for youth with LGBTQ parents is a real problem. As shown in the GLSEN report on the opposite page, some students with LGBTQ parents have transferred schools or dropped out completely as a result of feeling unsafe. Curricula and information about LGBTQ individuals and their families are still being banned from schools and libraries, and people are still actively trying to exclude us.

For example, in May 2005, the Oklahoma House of Representatives passed a bill (81-3) to ban books about gay families from the children's section of public and school libraries. In 2008, *Uncle Bobby's Wedding,* by Sarah Brannen, was passionately challenged at a Colorado library because it features a gay uncle who marries his partner. Luckily, the demand to ban it was denied. In 2005 in Troy, Michigan, school posters that read

Statistics from the GLSEN report

- 51% of youth with LGBTQ parents reported that they felt unsafe at school because of their perceived or actual sexual orientation, a personal characteristic, or because of their race/ethnicity. Of these, 23% felt unsafe due to their family makeup (i.e. having an LGBTQ parent) and 21% felt unsafe due to their perceived or actual sexual orientation.
- 65% of youth with LGBTQ parents frequently heard students use blatantly homophobic language such as "faggot" or "dyke." 17% heard these remarks made about their own families.
- 75% of youth with LGBTQ parents frequently heard students say "that's so gay" or "you're so gay"; expressions where "gay" is meant to mean something bad or devalued.
- Merely 38% of youth with LGBTQ parents reported that school staff frequently intervened when these biased remarks were made by students.
- 39% of youth with LGBTQ parents heard homophobic remarks being made by teachers and other school staff.
- Less than 48% of youth with LGBTQ parents who experienced harrassment or assault in school ever reported the events to school staff.
- More than 30% felt like they could not fully participate in school due to having an LGBTQ parent. 36% felt like teachers and other school staff ignored the fact that they had an LGBTQ parent, and 22% were blatantly discouraged from talking about having an LGBTQ parent.

GAY PEOPLE ARE EVERYDAY PEOPLE were vehemently protested by parents. (The school kept the posters intact.) Although we receive less attention, children living with gay parents often experience or witness anti-LGBTQ backlash and exclusion that is similar to that experienced by gay students.

Kids with LGBTQ parents are sometimes taunted when other students find out that they have a gay parent. Alexis, age eleven, from South Philly, thinks that she is the only person in school with lesbian parents and says that other students have referred to her as "nasty" simply because she has two mothers. She also gets teased because she speaks out about anti-gay slurs she hears at school. She tries to ignore them, but those attacks on her family hurt.

Some students with LGBTQ parents complain that others assume they're gay just because of their parents. Of course, it doesn't matter whether you happen

I'm being teased at school, but I don't want my parents to worry. What should I do?

Everyone is teased about something, but regardless of the reason, teasing is wrong and can be hurtful. There is also a difference between a little teasing and big, mean, nasty teasing. Either way, tell your parents so that they can give you advice. How can they support you at school if they don't know there's a problem? If you're concerned about making the situation worse, tell your parents not to parade up there like the parent patrol. If you refuse to tell your parent, you must tell a trusted teacher or the school counselor or disciplinarian. Otherwise, the teasing will probably continue.

to be gay like your parent, but it does matter if you get labeled or harassed by your classmates, especially if those people see being gay as a problem.

Unfortunately, some schools are downright unsupportive of LGBTQ families and have policies that penalize students with LGBTQ families. For example, in 2003, a second-grader named Marcus from Lafayette, Louisiana, was punished by his teacher for using the word "gay." Yet he wasn't using the word as an insult. He was simply telling a classmate that he had lesbian moms and used the word to explain what being gay meant. This caused an uproar at the school, all because Marcus was attempting to educate others about his family. These types of fallouts instill fear among LGBTQ families and make the academic climate feel unsafe. Lack of school support can also make many of us feel alone, distrustful, and defensive—and it can be a reason to decide to stay closeted.

In junior high and my early high school years, I was very active in extracurricular activities, including the journalism club, drama club, and Spanish club. I had a good group of friends and got great grades. I was a pretty normal adolescent, considered a feisty nerd, and I did not think about my mom being gay every day. I had a life outside of being the child of a lesbian. However, as well-adjusted as I thought I was, I recall getting into fights and arguments because people teased me for having a gay mother. On a weekly basis, I heard stupid anti-gay slurs, such as "bulldagger," "dyke," "faggot," "sissy," and the wildly popular "That's so gay," being thrown around. I witnessed gay students, and one of my favorite teachers (who was rumored to be gay), being bullied and made fun of—oftentimes behind their backs. It was just the way things were. These types of experiences make children with LGBTQ parents feel uncomfortable and/or bound to secrecy.

Will, age eighteen, from Yonkers, thinks that education is the key to resolving issues of discrimination and rejection of gays and children with LGBTQ parents. "I think schools should have clubs for and about gays to educate people so they'll know how to approach gays and not with the negativity. The more you know, the better you can deal with that person." He's definitely onto something with that, and lots of schools are already leaning in that direction.

In the '80s, Gay–Straight Alliances (GSAs) and Gay, Lesbian, and Straight Education Network (GLSEN) chapters were nearly unheard of. Today, there are more than 3,000 GSAs in middle and high schools across forty-nine states. Even with this progress, however, many LGBTQ students and students with LGBTQ parents are still fighting their way through school. Will, who shared his feelings about the importance of these types of groups, said that when he was in school, he fought a lot. "People would come in my face talking about my dads. They were homophobic, I guess. When I'd get into physical fights, putting people's heads into poles, I'd end up getting suspended. The staff would tell me to ignore comments and be the bigger person." Although Will went on to say that the staff at his school helped him to exercise better self-restraint, as the victim, he was the one who was being blamed for the fights—not the homophobic bullies.

ARE SCHOOLS SAFE ENOUGH?

Many schools now have zero-tolerance or anti-harassment policies. Some states even have laws that try to ensure a safe environment for all students. The 2005 GLSEN survey, *From Teasing to Torment: School Climate in America,* reported that 48 percent of secondary school students and 51 percent of teachers report that their school has an anti-harassment policy that specifically details how to handle discriminatory words and actions based on sexual orientation or gender identity/expression. The survey also reveals that the majority of teachers think schools should take responsibility to ensure these policies are followed. As a matter of fact, a whopping 73 percent of teachers strongly agree that they have an obligation to ensure a safe and supportive learning environment for LGBTQ students. Meanwhile, however, youth with LGBTQ parents, as shared in GLSEN's 2008 survey, do not think that teachers and school administration do enough to safeguard them.

Why the discrepancy? In some cases it's easy to profess a desire to protect students, but it's also quite likely that teachers aren't always around when discriminatory behavior is being played out among students. Teachers and administrators can't be within earshot of all student interactions. There are also some teachers who take on the "kids will be kids" attitude and allow comments like "That's so gay" slide. If we are going to truly safeguard our kids, it requires a zero-tolerance policy, even around slang that some people might not consider to be a big deal. The fact of the matter, however, is that these types of comments are not benign, and they amount to institutionalized discrimination.

Another factor is that there are some LGBTQ teachers who are afraid themselves about what could happen if the administration or students knew they were gay. Closeted teachers, who may be the ones with the most at stake when it comes to protecting gay students and students with gay parents, may inadvertently turn a blind eye so as not to get called out themselves. Adell, a middleschool teacher from Chicago, told me, "I'm not out at work because I'm scared; scared of losing my job or being treated differently or looked at differently. I just try to go with the flow, although I don't necessarily like doing that." When we have a school environment where even the teachers have to hide, it certainly doesn't bode well for the students.

Spencer, age eleven, lives in Denver with his recently divorced lesbian mother and attends a progressive and culturally diverse international school. Although he likes his school, he still feels that his school is "not really a safe place to talk about having gay parents" because "people talk really negative about gays at school." (Spencer's mother emailed me a few months after our interview and said that through their discussion of his fears, he now feels more comfortable talking about his family.) Aylesha, age twelve, and her brother Chris, age fifteen, attend school in Maryland. Both of them make it a point not to mention at school that they have a gay

> **When people say negative things about the LGBTQ community, my teacher never addresses it. What should I do?**
>
> Try to talk to your teacher in private and tell him or her how this lack of action makes you feel. If your teacher doesn't improve, inform your parent who may need to talk to the teacher and/or the principal. Teachers must be held accountable for creating a safe, comfortable learning environment for all of their students.

father, although they state that they are proud of their family and that they feel comfortable at their schools.

Safety and feeling as if you belong are important. Some students just don't feel comfortable talking about their families at school because they do not want to experience any backlash or unnecessary stress. All students have the right to feel comfortable and embraced at their schools, regardless of any differences. *Welcoming Children from Sexual-Minority Families into Our Schools*, by Linda and Laurel Lamme (a fabulous mom-and-daughter duo), cites the results of an Australian study about the experiences of children with an LGBTQ parent. This study shows that kids' experiences vary depending on grade level and the type of school (public versus private). In early school years, students are very open about their parents, but by middle school, they begin to hear negative things about gays, and they close up. In the early high school years, things are usually still pretty rough, but by the middle of high school, students tend to become more comfortable and open about being from a sexual-minority family. The next section will discuss the different challenges in middle and high school.

MIDDLE SCHOOL CHALLENGES

"It is interesting to me how in today's culture in the schools, no teacher, no faculty member, and no student would tolerate hatred toward another person based on appearance of race, religion, or class, and yet when it comes to sexual orientation, we as a community tend to permit this verbal abuse. Every day in school, some sort of discrimination, whether intentional or not, is experienced and directed at the LGBTQ community. 'Don't be such a fag.' 'That's so gay!' These words, although extremely offensive, have been absorbed into everyday slang," says Sarah, age seventeen, from San Francisco.

Though Sarah is in high school now, she feels like the worst of this type of discrimination was in middle school. Middle school is typically when you learn that being "gay" is a bad thing. Think back to the first time you heard "That's so gay" or someone being referred to as "gay," meaning something dumb, ridiculous, or undesirable. Chances are you heard it early on in your school career. (My own daughter came home from school one day in the first grade telling me that one of her classmates had called her "gay.")

That was the case for Desiree, age thirteen, who often hears homophobic remarks at her Chicago school. When I interviewed her, it was obvious how conflicted she felt about being part of an LGBTQ household. While she is very close to her family and clearly loves her lesbian moms and five siblings very much, she also has a hard time dealing with the kids at school who talk badly about her for having lesbian moms. It's all the more prevalent for her because her moms are very active at the school and are therefore quite visible.

Desiree's little sister, Kiara, age eleven, already identifies as queer and is very confident about who she is, but even she experiences teasing at school, both because of her moms and her own sexual and gender identity. Whether it's discussed or not, school is usually the most difficult place for pre-teens and teens with gay parents. Unfortunately, middle school youth can be vicious and mean. It's not just your school—it's all over. We

I hear "That's so gay" or some other anti-gay comment every day. I don't want to sound ridiculous by calling everyone out on their stupidity. What should I do?

Most of us don't want to rock the boat. You should address homophobia, but don't be a jerk about it. You'll only irritate those around you and then they lose the point. Don't fight every battle—only the important ones. Also, educate enough people so that you aren't alone in changing the way your peers see the LGBTQ community.

don't know why folks hit puberty and lose their minds, but it does happen, and youth with LGBTQ parents often fall prey to this rampant meanness. It totally sucks, but it's totally true. But don't be discouraged, because things typically get better as you get older. Until then, protect yourself and reach out to supports and teachers to limit this kind of foul behavior. Also, try to contribute to the solution. Part of the reason why bullying in middle school is so intense is that kids tease others—even their friends—to avoid being made fun of themselves, or to draw attention away from their own problems. Don't fall into this trap. Be an ally to other students, and you might find that they will return the favor someday.

AM I HOMOPHOBIC?

Sometimes, you may hear anti-gay slurs dribble from your own lips. "That is soooo gay!" *Oops, did I say that?* Some of us with LGBTQ parents use the same anti-LGBTQ language and name-calling that hurts our feelings in an attempt to remain closeted about our parents or to fit in with others, or just because we hear it so often that it becomes part of our normal vocabulary. I can remember teasing effeminate boys in school by saying that they had "sugar in their tank," or calling them "suspect" (both meaning that I suspected they were gay because of their mannerisms). It took me a long time to understand internalized homophobia and heterosexism, so it also took me a long time to erase these phrases from my vocabulary.

I know that some youth with an LGBTQ parent fall into similar patterns. It's not until someone breaks down the destructive effects of using derogatory slang that we are generally motivated to stop. And even when we know better, we still may fall victim to using anti-gay language. Will admits, "I ain't gon' lie. I say 'faggot' sometimes too, but I try not to because when you think about it, it's like disrespecting my father and what he is."

A lot of kids may feel like it's not a big deal to make fun of gays or to use slurs that are heard everyday on school grounds. They may even make anti-gay comments and notice that they don't feel anything. This is not justification for continuing on with business as usual. This probably means that this person has become hardened to the effects of this kind of language, to the point that they just don't feel it anymore. Don't allow yourself to become that person.

You might also feel like you're justified in using slang or disparaging language because you are part of a queer household. You may feel like this is your territory, and that if you say, "That's so gay," or "You're a fag," you get a free pass. If you get angry when "outsiders" use the same language against you or toward individuals you love, but then feel like you get to use that same language because you're part of that community, think again. We see this logic in the black community as well, when blacks refer to each other as "niggas," or when folks who are closely aligned to the black community use this slang even if they're not black. Just like the word "faggot," this term has roots in oppression. It's important to tread carefully and not to propagate something that's actually quite hurtful to our communities.

In March 2007, a student at a Santa Rosa high school was written up for saying "That's so gay" after other students asked her if she had ten moms because of her Mormon background. The school wrote her up because of their district policy to protect gay students from harassment. This young lady claimed that she was not trying to attack or insult gays, she just uses that term to mean "stupid," "silly," and "dumb." Her parents have since filed a lawsuit against the school for writing up their daughter for the use of what they deemed to be a "popular term." This is a good example of what happens when bigots are tolerated just because certain terms and phrases are commonplace.

Discrimination is wrong always. Fighting fire with fire is not the best way to defuse a situation. If this student wanted to say, "You guys are stupid and ignorant about your knowledge of the Mormon faith," then that's what she should have said. We all have to be more conscious of the terminology we use, whether it's "that's so gay" or "no homo," and look at the underlying, discriminatory implications. It is easy to be lured into anti-gay behavior (i.e., picking on seemingly gay kids, using the word "gay" as an insult, snickering when you see a transgender student), but we have to check ourselves and keep a handle on our own homophobia. Due to a long cultural history of homophobia and anti-gay sentiments, some people believe that everyone has internalized homophobia on some level. I think we're finally getting to a place in some parts of the country and among certain populations where this is no longer the case, but take this short quiz to determine your level of internal homophobia and comfort level with having LGBTQ parents.

HOLY HOMOPHOBIA!

Let's be real. Everyone has different comfort and tolerance levels when it comes to having gay parents. Some of us make an annual appearance at Pride, while others of us wouldn't go if we were offered a million bucks. Wherever you fall along the spectrum, it's okay to be exactly where you are. This quiz isn't designed to judge you. The goal is to make you more aware of your feelings and thoughts about your family situation. Circle the answer that best fits you and how you feel.

1. Have you ever used the term "That's so gay"?

    a. Of course, who doesn't?

    b. Never! It's totally wrong.

    c. Sometimes, but I try not to.

2. How do you feel about gay marriage?

    a. It doesn't matter to me.

    b. I think it's great and have already written my letter to President Obama asking him to support gay marriage.

    c. Marriage is between a man and a woman. Period.

3. What would you do if you saw a gay person being harassed?

    a. That's not my problem. I've got my own troubles.

    b. Ask him or her if they are okay afterwards.

    c. Jump in on the action and help that person.

4. When one of your friends says something negative about gays, you:

    a. Teach them about tolerance and start singing "We Are the World."

    b. Stay quiet.

    c. Applaud them for their honesty and chime in with your own two cents about those darn gays.

5. When your parent first came out, you thought:

    a. Oh my God, what is this going to do to my social life?

    b. Who cares? Can I borrow the car?

    c. I'm not sure how I felt about this and I'm still mulling it over.

6. Have you ever been to a gay pride parade?

    a. Of course, it's a family tradition.

    b. I wouldn't be caught dead there.

    c. I've been to Pride, but guys in drag aren't my thing.

7. If a random kid from school asked you if your mom was gay, you'd respond:

    a. Yeah, why?

    b. None of your business.

    c. No. (Lying, of course.)

8. In your opinion, Rosie O'Donnell is:

    a. Too butch.

    b. A good show host, but a little old for my taste.

    c. A genius for co-founding the R Family cruise.

9. If your gay parent and their partner showed up at parent–teacher conference night, you'd:

    a. Get them both some cookies and juice and hope this kind gesture takes the emphasis off your failing gym grade.

    b. Pretend like you don't know them because your mom looks dorky in her work outfit.

    c. That would never happen because you would never allow them both to show up at the same time.

10. How many gays outside of your parent(s) and their friends do you associate with?

    a. And ruin my reputation? Pul-leaze.

    b. Some of my friends are gay.

    c. I've lost count.

Use the answer key to tally your points.

Question	a.	b.	c.
1.	2	1	3
2.	1	2	3
3.	1	3	2
4.	2	1	3
5.	3	2	1
6.	1	3	2
7.	1	2	3
8.	3	2	1
9.	1	2	3
10.	3	2	1

TOTAL 10–16: WHOLE MILK

You are totally about human rights and equality for all people. You are probably more of an activist than your parent (even if it has nothing to do with LGBTQ issues). You can come off like Mother Teresa at times, so choose your battles and stop preaching to everyone within your reach. Folks don't want to hear about equal rights at the swim meet. Just swim the doggone race. You are a great LGBTQ family advocate, and the world needs more humanitarians like you. (Note: Even the best-intentioned people sometimes deal with internalized homophobia as well, so don't think you're completely off the hook. It's a process.)

TOTAL 17–23: SOY MILK

You are pretty accepting of others. It's true that it's a process to examine our own internalized homophobia, and you're working on it. Overall, you don't have a problem with gays, but you might feel like it's easier to just pretend like your family is totally straight because it's a lot less complicated. Sometimes you don't speak out and advocate as much as you could, and you may have a little fear about stepping up in public. That takes time and comfort. Find battles worth fighting and speak out against all injustice. If we don't speak out on behalf of our families, who will?

TOTAL 24–30: RICE MILK

You might be uncomfortable with having an LGBTQ parent or about LGBTQ issues in general. It's okay. We all have our path and our process. You may want to figure out why you are so triggered by gays and talk through it openly and honestly with your parent or another adult support. You may need to seek counseling for an objective, nonemotional ear to hear you out so you can understand the root of what's bothering you and maybe get to a place where it's ultimately easier for you to be a little more open about your family situation.

TOUGHING IT OUT IN HIGH SCHOOL

For most of middle school, I didn't share with anyone about my mother being gay. It was easy to hide because I was living with my father at the time. By high school, I had moved in with my mother, and her outright defiance of stereotypical gender roles became a problem for me. The neighborhood kids would see my mother in the streets with no bra on under her T-shirt and talk about it in school. Worse, as a construction worker, she wore dusty work boots, a hard hat, and dirt as daily attire, so my friends joked about it all the time. My peers often referred to her as "sir" (as did unsuspecting store clerks). Because I knew who I was by high school, I didn't care as much as I did when I was in middle school, but it still upset me. And I found that I was more bothered with my mom than I was with my peers. She got on my nerves—a lot. Therefore, we had run-ins often.

For some of us, reaching high school means being in more conflict with our parent(s) than ever before. They will irritate you more. They will crowd your space and screw up your chi. This is pretty normal for a lot of parents

People think I'm gay because my parents are. How should I handle this?

Arguing about your sexual orientation does two things: (1) It subconsciously says that being homosexual is wrong or else you wouldn't be arguing that you aren't. (2) It gives the other person your power. If you know you're not gay, don't get into those dumb arguments. Who cares whether you are gay or not? Tell the idiot with no business of his own to get a clue, and continue to be who you are. Don't try to play football (if you hate it) just to seem more masculine, and don't sleep with half of the football team to prove that you're not a lesbian. Just be you—whatever that entails.

and kids around this time in life. Parents and teens fight. It has nothing to do with having an LGBTQ parent. It's age-appropriate behavior. It's part of the journey of self-discovery. You are gaining more independence, or at least searching for it. Parents sometimes don't understand this, or they do understand but want to limit what you can and can't do. This is sometimes totally justified, and sometimes it can be a little overprotective. Use those great communication skills and try to resolve conflict with your parents in a responsible, mature manner.

High school is a time when many teens develop their own personalities and figure out who they are. Usually, we are less concerned with our parents and more interested in our own lives. Like Hope, you're probably trying to figure yourself out and separate your identity from that of your parents. This is also the time when some teens explore their gender and sexual identity. These things are generally more complex when you're the child of a gay person.

Orson, age thirty-two and son of a gay father, reflects on some of the challenges he faced in high school: "As I got into puberty, my peer relationships were more important. I started dating women and began having a little bit of a hard time with my father. I wanted a traditional father, whatever that meant. I wanted a father who could talk to me about girls and football." Will also shared the ways in which having a gay father made him question his own sexuality more intensely: "I used to think because my dad was gay and I was surrounded by gay guys that I would be gay too. I used to think I had something to prove, grabbing on this girl's arm and that girl's arm. But then I realized that I have nothing to prove. My dad is who he is, and I am who I am."

The teenage years are usually the period where questions and reactions around sexuality come up the most. I too remember being confused about my sexuality during that time in my life. There were rumors floating around high school about me being a lesbian because my mother was gay and because I wasn't sexually active. This rumor got started by guys who were harassing me because I was a virgin. After a while, I bought into those rumors and began thinking that my abstinence was indeed a sign that I might be gay. It didn't matter that I had never crushed on Janet Jackson or any other woman. What mattered to me and my peers was what I *appeared* to be on the exterior. The rumors were hurtful, but it was again because of this implication that there was something wrong with being gay—which was a direct implication that there was something wrong with my mom.

Some of the students I interviewed were much more progressive and self-accepting than I was about my sexuality. "Up until high school, I identified as straight so my parents addressed me in a hetero context. When I began questioning in late high school and emerged as queer, my parents understood where I was coming from. My overall identity is still something I'm exploring. It's a process," says Hope, who's just recently graduated from high school.

Along with being comfortable about who you are comes added responsibility and self-exploration. This usually involves doing things that you've never done before, and it can also involve coming into your own—being more comfortable because you're starting to understand yourself and where you fit in your own environment better than you ever have. Most of the youth and young adults I surveyed became comfortable telling people about their families in high school and college. They became more comfortable because they realized that having LGBTQ parents didn't really matter and that this diversity added to who they were as people. Most high school–aged students interviewed for this book didn't have a problem with their friends when they came out about having an LGBTQ parent, but a few did.

Alissa, the twenty-nine-year-old daughter of a bisexual woman, explains what happened when she was "outed" at her all-girl Catholic school: "I had a best friend, and she was one of the only people outside of my family who I allowed into my personal life. When she would spend the night, she'd see my mom and her girlfriend sleep in the same room. One night, I spent the night over at her house and she tried to do some [sexual] stuff to me, and I wouldn't let her. She used that against me and told the whole school about my mother. I was devastated. I ended up transferring to a boarding school out of state to get away from it all, including my mother and her girlfriend." This is an example of an unfortunate situation where Alissa's best friend assumed that Alissa was a lesbian because of her mom. She used Alissa to explore her own curiosity about her sexuality, and then, after being rejected, "outed" Alissa in a very punishing way. She likely did this to hurt, demean, and silence Alissa for not going along with her advances.

Although LGBTQ parent-related drama like this may not be common, sometimes sticky situations like the above will arise. You will be more resilient and able to deal with situations like this if you have a strong support system in place and if the school is doing its job. Most important, you can strategize with mentors and others like yourself about the best ways to avoid confrontations in school and create an environment conducive to learning. After all, that's what school is about. In the next chapter, you will take a fun quiz to grade how LGBTQ-friendly your school is and receive tips on handling homophobia and isolation at your school.

OUR**VOICES**

WHAT HAVE YOU LEARNED, FOR THE BETTER OR THE WORSE, FROM HAVING A GAY PARENT?

It doesn't matter if you're gay or not. Just be who you are and follow your heart.

—ASHLEE, 12

People aren't always accepting of minorities, and I've learned that you have to be accepting of everyone, even if they can't accept you. Good friends don't care what orientation your parents are; they only care about you. Family is not made only by blood and marriage. Your family should consist of those who care for you most.

—JAMIE, 18

I have learned to look at life differently. I do not have any prejudices towards anyone. Everyone is created equal and just because you have gay parents or your skin color is different does not mean anything. My mom has taught me a lot throughout my life. She taught me how to be strong and independent.

—ELIZABETH, 16

I have learned that there are a lot of closed-minded people in this world. You have to be careful of them. There are two choices; either stand up to them or hide from them. Recently, I've begun to stand up more, but when I was younger, I found it easier to keep my silence.

—AMY, 17

That the pursuit of being yourself is the most important thing any of us can reach for. I know my dad wouldn't have torn apart our family for anything other than something that was critical to his survival. I learned I can deal with any challenge life throws at me.

—SARAH, 26

RECONCILEFORCLAIRE

by Hannah Farnsworth, 19

I wanted to be part of a normal family
Free from difficulties
And prejudice;
A life where I could blend in.
Having two mums can screw you up —
The impact of society
I planned to be free from the torture
To move away from that which hurt me.
Until I realized
That the freedom I thought I wanted
Came at too high a price.
I was not willing to pay.
So I let go of my fears
And entered the community,
For myself, as myself.
Reconciliation with my heart,
As I realized that I would allow
My children to endure
That which I had vowed they would not.

This poem was first published in *Focus on MY Family: A Queerspawn Anthology*, created by the COLAGE Youth Leadership and Action Program.

THE**EXPERT'S**JOURNAL**PAGES**

SOURCES

John Cloud, "The Battle Over Gay Teens," *Time*, October 2005, pg. 42.

J. G. Kosciw and E. M. Diaz, *Involved, Invisible, Ignored: The Experiences of Lesbian, Gay, Bisexual and Transgender Parents and Their Children in Our Nation's K–12 Schools.* (New York: GLSEN, 2008).

Josh Arterovis, "Won't Somebody Think of the Children," *ProudParenting.com*, 2005, www.proudparenting.com.

Jim Brown, "Michigan Parents Protest Pro-Homosexual Posters on Public School Campus," Agape Press, American Family Association, June 2005, http://headlines.agapepress.org/archive/6/afa/22005c.asp.

Harris Interactive and GLSEN, *From Teasing to Torment: School Climate in America, A Survey of Students and Teahers* (New York: GLSEN, 2005).

Linda and Laurel Lamme, "Welcoming Children from Sexual-Minority Families into Our Schools," (Bloomington, IN: Phi Delta Kappa Educational Foundation, Fastback 507, 2003).

Sarah Gogin, "A Safe Place," COLAGE, www.colage.org/gallery/creative/safe_place.htm.

"'That's So Gay' Prompts a Lawsuit," Associated Press, February 28, 2007, www.msnbc.msn.com/id/17388702/.

Chapter Five

How to **Survive** School

"It is not who you attend school with but who controls the school you attend."
—Nikki Giovanni, poet

Since school is so often a place of high drama, I thought it would be important to provide sound advice on how to create the most positive academic experience possible during the many years you're going to be there. It's not enough to just talk about the problems that exist. We have to find the best solutions and ways of handling all kinds of things—from quips to mean-spiritedness to bullying and more. First, I will share a few tips on making your life better at school and among your peers. Then you'll have an opportunity to grade your own school by taking a quiz called Does Your School

Make the Grade? At the end of this chapter, we'll talk about ways we can all improve the academic environment, one school at a time.

1. Be proud of your individuality. Before anything else, you are an individual, with your own thoughts, feelings, and experiences. Although you may share many similarities with your peers and friends, such as favorite music, fashion, food, or television shows, you are also unique. You may be a racial minority, or you might be the only male feminist, fighting chauvinists daily. There is always something that will make you stand apart—and that's a good thing. It's our similarities *and* our diversity that make the world a rich, complex, and stimulating place. So be yourself and stand proud. Your parent is gay or your dad is a woman—so what? It only adds texture to your life. Now you have a different perspective to share with the world.

2. Don't allow other people's ignorance to taint your personal beliefs. Many of us have been told that our parent's homosexuality or transgender status is wrong, which implies, on some level, that our existence is unacceptable as well. We hear this underlying message every time we're subjected to an anti-gay remark, or when a teacher or other authority figure asks us who our "real mom" or "real dad" is. Don't let these realities sidetrack you from being you. You have to listen to your heart, use common sense, and filter out the nonsense. It may take more effort, but you have to think for yourself, make your own decisions, and live your life with love, compassion, and purpose.

3. Immediately address any negative feelings or fears with your parents or another adult you trust. It is okay to feel weird about your parent loving a person of the same gender. It is not okay to keep these feelings bottled inside. If you fail to deal with your feelings, they will spill over into everything else, negatively affecting your school performance and social life. It may be stressful and strained at first, but you have to communicate with your parent(s). You may even have to take the initiative, because some parents may be clueless about you even having any issues regarding their homosexuality, especially if you've never spoken up. Elements of effective communication include listening, attempting to understand other perspectives, organizing your thoughts, and being respectful.

4. Let others know when they have offended you. Some people say the craziest things. Sometimes it stems from trying to get a rise out of you, and other times it's because they really don't know any better. Speaking up when people say hurtful things can be a therapeutic and empowering experience. It can also be a teachable moment for the other person. Use your personal and unique experience as an opportunity to educate, challenge, and inform others about our families. Speak out against injustices and report to school administrators and to your parents any discriminatory practices carried out by teachers and students.

5. Find outlets and resources that reflect our families. A number of written materials, documentaries, and Internet resources for and about children living in sexual-minority families are now available. It is important that we support media that address our issues and show real portrayals of our families. Rainbow Rumpus (www.rainbowrumpus.org), a fabulous website for younger kids with LGBTQ parents (it does not have quite as much content for teens) and Two Lives Publishing (www.twolives.com), a cool website where you can purchase relevant books, are both great places to find resources that feature families like yours.

6. Develop a support system. Too many of us have no idea that there are many other children with gay parents. We often feel lonely and voiceless. You can create a strong support system by hanging with the kids of your parents' gay friends and making friends with other kids of gay parents or anyone you know who's out at school—peers or teachers. You can also form alliances at school that can consist of other kids with gay parents, gay students, and open-minded teachers and students. Schools with formal Gay–Straight Alliances tend to have more support from administration and safer environments for gay students and children with gay parents. Ask your school administrators if they have safe-zone or zero tolerance policies, or inquire about what steps have been taken to support students from sexual-minority families. By doing this, you create an awareness for administrators about the less visible demographics of the school population and hold them accountable for creating a safe space for all students. One of the most inclusive places you will find support is COLAGE. Go to their website to find chapters in your area. If there aren't any, check out their online resources, their *Just for Us* publication, and their pen pal program.

Although these basic tips may not solve all of your school and peer dilemmas, they will support you in becoming more confident, honest, and vocal about your needs, feelings, and thoughts.

DOES YOUR SCHOOL MAKE THE GRADE?

Our schools constantly grade us, making sure that we are up to par. Now it's time to turn the tables and judge your school. This section is for those of you who know that your school can use a little work as it relates to understanding, accepting, and learning about students from LGBTQ-parented families. Let's test our schools to see how knowledgeable and safe they are at this point. Take this short quiz to see if your school made honor roll or whether it needs some serious tutoring.

1. Is there an LGBTQ student club of any type or a group that promotes diversity at your school?

    a. Yes

    b. No

2. Are there any visible LGBTQ teachers or staff at your school?

    a. Yes

    b. No

3. Are there books and curricula that help you to learn about LGBTQ families and LGBTQ individuals?

    a. Yes

    b. No

4. Have you witnessed or experienced LGBTQ students or students with LGBTQ parents being teased, harassed, or assaulted?

    a. Yes

    b. No

5. Do you have any supportive adults at your school who you could talk to (if necessary) about having a gay parent?

    a. Yes

    b. No

6. Are there any extracurricular activities that focus on the lives of LGBTQ individuals (i.e., Day of Silence, Gay Prom, etc.) at your school?

    a. Yes

    b. No

7. Do school forms and literature use inclusive language (i.e., "parent" instead of "mother" and "father")?

    a. Yes

    b. No

8. Do you know of other students with LGBTQ parents at the school?

    a. Yes

    b. No

9. Do you know of policies at your school that are designed to protect LGBTQ individuals and students with LGBTQ parents?

    a. Yes

    b. No

10. Is your school a designated safe zone, complete with visible posters, stickers, and staff contacts?

 a. Yes

 b. No

Use this answer key to tally your points.

POINT SYSTEM:	
1. a. = 1	b. = 0
2. a. = 1	b. = 0
3. a. = 1	b. = 0
4. a. = 0	b. = 1
5. a. = 1	b. = 0
6. a. = 1	b. = 0
7. a. = 1	b. = 0
8. a. = 1	b. = 0
9. a. = 1	b. = 0
10. a. = 1	b. = 0

TOTAL 0–2 = GRADE F

The F here does not stand for fabulous. Your school truly needs to step up its game. Your place of learning is not doing a good enough job to create a safe, affirming environment for LGBTQ students and students with LGBTQ parents.

Your school needs anti-bias and diversity training quick, fast, and in a hurry! Go to the Human Rights Campaign website (www.hrc.org) to find a list of diversity trainers in your area.

While on the road to becoming more inclusive, your school may need a little more direction regarding its policies. Direction needs to come from the top, and school administrators need to know what is at stake. Go to the pros at the American Civil Liberties Union (www.aclu.org). They have a great Lesbian and Gay Rights section that provides legal advice and success stories of schools that are doing things well. The ACLU also shares free copies of their resources to improve LGBTQ equality and decrease discrimination in our schools. COLAGE has posters, movies, tips for administrators and teachers, and a plethora of other resources. The positive note is that your school can only go up from here. Good luck in creating change!

TOTAL 2–3 = GRADE D

Knowledge is power, but your school couldn't beat Superman pumped full of Kryptonite. It is doing a poor job helping others to understand us and protecting LGBTQ students and students with LGBTQ families. Added curricula, visibility, and events supporting LGBTQ groups may help your school shine. For a listing of great books and media about youth with LGBTQ parents, go to the COLAGE website (www.colage.org) and check out the resource section at the end of this book. Tell your school librarian to get on the ball and order these books and films for students and teachers to use as classroom and personal resources. In Spring 2003, COLAGE's Youth and Action Program created a fabulous guide called *Tips for Making Classrooms Safer for Students with Lesbian, Gay, Bisexual, and Transgender Parents*. There is also a guide called *Preventing Prejudice: Lesson Plan Guide for Elementary Schools*, which may work if you are in middle school. Both of these documents offer great suggestions on how your school can start improving its climate. You can also go to www.safeschoolscoalition.org to get great posters, stickers, and other resources to upgrade your school environment. Help your school get on track!

TOTAL 4–5 = GRADE C

Now, when you bring C grades home (unless you're coming up from F land), you can still expect to get an earload from your parents, right? "Couldn't you have worked a little harder in history, honey?" or "Why don't you do a few extra assignments to get some extra credit?" The same applies here. Your school is doing a mediocre job at creating a bias-free environment, which means they're also doing a mediocre job of promoting all types of diversity.

Your school has to work a little harder to enter the hall of greatness. LGBTQ-related activities, safe zones, and added visibility are in order. Join or create a Gay–Straight Alliance at your school and contact GLSEN (Gay, Lesbian, and Straight Education Network) at www.glsen.org for more advice and support. Another cool resource for administrators and teachers at your school is Meredith Maran's *50 Ways to Support Lesbian and Gay Equality*. This book features dozens of essays by celebrities, politicians, LGBTQ allies, and parents just like yours and mine. Thought-provoking essays such as "Acknowledge Heterosexism," by Julie Bloch, "Take On the Pronoun Challenge (But Don't Lose Sleep Over It)," by Noelle Howey, and "Choose Your Words With Cuidado," by Daisy Hernandez, give simple solutions for supporting equality in your area. Check it out! Your local school council should also have LGBTQ parents represented in its membership. They will make sure that equality issues are addressed and have the clout to make change happen. With just a little more direction, C schools can easily transform into honor roll stars. Your school just needs to keep moving forward to see more success.

TOTAL 6–8 = GRADE B

Your school is doing a good job at supporting its LGBTQ students and students with LGBTQ parents. There are probably a significant number of visible LGBTQ families and students at your school. Visibility is good. Visibility brings attention. Attention brings forward challenges to be addressed. Addressing challenges stirs up action. Action brings about change. Your school knows this and has taken actions to support its school policies and families.

Now it's time to take it to the next level: organizing. The supa-dupa fly Gay–Straight Alliance Network is based in California, but it provides resources for people in all locales through its totally progressive website, www.gsanetwork.org (they now are helping to start other state-based GSA networks, and in doing so, are substantially widening their national reach). The materials teach you how to have an awesome GSA by knowing your legal rights, developing leadership, fundraising, increasing your membership, sponsoring fun events, and much more! The GSA Network website will also teach you how to plan successful events such as Trans

Day of Remembrance. They also have brain-food pages to help you think more critically, with documents such as "What Every Super-Rad Straight Ally Should Know" and "Building Anti-Racist GSAs." Your school is doing great. Now it's time to fine-tune and build on the foundation.

TOTAL 9–10 = GRADE A

Your school has made it onto the honor roll! It should be ranked summa cum laude in the fight for LGBTQ equality, and you are a lucky duck. I personally wish I had attended schools like yours when I was your age. You can be yourself without fear of repercussion, harassment, or embarrassment. Your school can be used as a model for how schools should look for LGBTQ families and students. Hopefully, your zone of higher learning is just as progressive when it comes to issues of race, gender, and class. Equality cannot be effective in a bubble. Your school should be aggressive about supporting all of its minority students, whether those are racial minorities or bilingual, disabled, working class, or transgender students. Schools supporting diversity means schools supporting people and their right to be different. Go shake your principal's hand for a job well done and keep an eye on how your school can improve even more. Striving for excellence is never a bad thing.

RESPONSIBLE ACTIONS TO TAKE

STUDENTS

1. **Get involved.** Tanya Mayo, former program director at the GSA Network, advises students, "Get active!! Start a GSA. Report it. Often people think it will make more trouble if they report teasing and harassment, but if you report it to a school administrator, coupled with doing some education and activism on campus, it helps put the issue on the table. Oftentimes people are afraid of things they don't understand, and once LGBTQ topics and issues are incorporated into the school climate, things will improve. You will also build allies and even have some fun starting a new club on campus."

You can also write your principal and suggest ways to make your school safer and more inclusive. There are no guarantees that things will change immediately, but you can set the ball in motion. Generations of students who follow you will be grateful!

2. **Educate yourself beyond the school curriculum.** Don't rely on it completely to inform you about the world. If you see a television show or news stories that relate to our families (and the class subject), mention it to your teacher as a possible addition to the curriculum.

3. **Speak out and educate others at school.** As a high school teacher, I constantly chastise my students about homophobia and their anti-gay remarks. One of the most powerful moments in one of my classrooms, however, didn't come from me. It happened when one of my students quietly said, "My dad is gay too, and I don't like it when y'all talk like that. It pisses me off." This all-African-American class was shocked that this student had a gay parent and a chain reaction occurred. Another female student came out to the class and then several more students felt comfortable enough to tell the class that they had gay family members. The conversation went from, "Yuck, I can't stand faggots" to "Wow, I didn't know your parent was gay too." The students finally began to engage in meaningful dialogue and debate about homosexuality. Speaking up works. It doesn't work every single time, but if you never try, chances are slim that the ne"gay"tivity will ever change. Your voice is powerful. Use it.

There's a rumor at school that my parents are gay. What should I do?

It's not a rumor if it's true. When I heard that same rumor about my mom, I flat out denied it. Guess what? They found out anyway. The majority didn't mind or care, but of course, there were a few bigots. Unless it is truly unsafe to be out about your parent, I don't advise you to lie. It takes up too much energy to keep up the lie. Just say something like, "Yeah, so what? What business is that of yours?" That way, you tell the truth, but put them in their place at the same time. Your parent's life, homosexual or not, is none of your classmates' business or concern.

SCHOOL STAFF

1. **Take personal responsibility for making your school's climate safe, comfortable, and non-biased.** Denise Wolk, director of publications for Educators for Social Responsibility, has several easily applied pointers for educators. "Becoming involved in programs like 'No Name Calling Week' can help address the issue of overall bullying in a school community. Setting up peer mediation programs can provide a student-centered opportunity to resolve differences and train kids to become allies for one another. It's important to examine our own beliefs as adults too—the principal of my kids' middle school was very supportive, but the assistant principal and many of the teachers were very prejudiced against my kids and that made it even more difficult for them. As a result, I also encourage mandatory professional development on diversity training for all school personnel (including PE and library staff). The fact is that many of our kids are living in 'alternative' family configurations, and it is vital to their social and emotional health to be supported by the professional adults in their lives."

2. **Make diversity part of your school's culture.** Interweave anti-bias curriculum and resources, mandatory cultural diversity teacher training, and inclusive language into the culture of your school and classrooms in a meaningful, seamless, and non-marginalized manner.

3. **Meet and develop a relationship with LGBTQ parents.** According to Linda and Laurel Lamme, authors of *Welcoming Children from Sexual-Minority Families into Our Schools*, "an important step toward school improvement is for teachers and administrators to become comfortable interacting with sexual-minority individuals."

4. **Research information about sexual-minority families as a way to educate yourself and your students** (even if you are not aware of any students from sexual-minority families at the school).

5. **Immediately address anti-LGBTQ behaviors, situations, and comments from students and other staff,** *and* ensure that disciplinary action follows. Policies are only as good as the teachers and administrators willing to back them up.

TIPS FOR PARENTS

1. **Research the school before you enroll your child.** Look into their policies and figure out what protections are in place. Denise Wolk strongly recommends that parents "speak with the principal and counseling staff about their family situation and provide a safety net for their kids *before* bullying happens—that way the kids know who to turn to when it happens."

2. **Be willing to be visible at your child's school.** It's not about being "outed." It's about being able to support your child, to create a safe school environment as a parent advocate of sexual-minority families, and to effect change.

3. **Volunteer at the school.** This creates more visibility and allows you to be a potential resource/role model for teachers and students.

4. **Reach out to other LGBTQ parents, develop working relationships with the school staff, and create a gay parent group with other parents at your child's school.** You also may want to create a Google group for LGBTQ parents that discusses school, coming out to your children, and other pertinent issues.

5. **Stay connected.** Talk with your child often about what goes on at school so that you can keep track of what's going on. Respect the choices that your child makes about when and how to come out about your family. Discuss these choices as a family to make sure that everyone is comfortable with them.

OUR**VOICES**

WHERE DO YOU GO TO RECEIVE SUPPORT?

"I receive support from different groups like COLAGE.*"*

—**ZAJI, 12**

"My sister—we talk if we need to but I don't really need much support. I don't think there is anything wrong with my mom, just how people in our society look upon her lifestyle."

—**AMY, 17**

"For support, I would go to my parents sometimes, and I would call up some of my very good friends that I have made from P-Town [Family Week event sponsored by COLAGE*]. They have really helped over the years."*

—**KEOTT, 16**

"The guidance counselor at my school."

—**ELAINA, 11**

"My family is a great support system. Nobody knows how difficult the situation is better than they do. Some of my gay friends are helpful too since they know what it's like to be [hated] and they won't judge me or my family for being 'different.'"

—**LORNE, 15**

THE**PICTURE**

by Sara Berger, 19, from her personal poetry collection

I'm wondering how much time has passed
As I sit here in my dorm
Looking at our picture.
I've got your eyes. You know it.
And a slightly crooked smile
To match yours.
I wish I had your cheekbones . . .
I wish I had your courage.
Though I've yet to find
The gay side
That you have,
Which I probably won't,
I believe we're very much alike
In all the ways that should count.
And although your lover,
She doesn't share
The same genes
Or blue jeans
As me,
I am convinced that I have her brainy wit . . .
Which is better than genetics anyway.
And it's a shame
That people can't tell
From the faces in the frame
All that we've been through . . .
All that we share.
And as I watch the airbrushed photo
Slowly collect with the dust
Almost always correlated to a lazy college student,
I remember the hoarse laughter,

Pig Latin,
Dancing in the living room,
Tears,
Rainbow flags,
The lookout,
Ellen,
And British Columbia . . .
And I remember how because of you and her,
My life was destined to be different.
Destined to be strange.
Hated.
Feared.
Queer.
And I remember how I would never change it for the world.

THE**EXPERT'S**JOURNAL**PAGES**

Chapter Six

Through **God's** Eyes

"If your spiritual philosophy is not moving you to the state of peace, wealth,
and love your spirit desires . . . you need a new spiritual philosophy."
— Sun Bear, Native American medicine man and author
(from *Acts of Faith*, by Iyanla Vanzant)

In its most loving state, religion is a powerful tool that helps us to learn acceptance, compassion, selflessness, and love. Some people use religion to communicate with a higher power, to make sense of the world around them, or to affirm their core beliefs. Others use religion as a tool to find inner peace and to promote social justice.

Unfortunately, sometimes people use religion to judge people, or to be mean and disrespectful to others.

LGBTQ individuals and their families have a long history of conflict with various religions because of rejection by the religious traditions they were brought up in. Usually, the forces that protest against our families most passionately are mainstream organized religious groups. Therefore, it can be hard for us as individuals from LGBTQ families to connect with organized religion. This is the case for Jamie, age eighteen, who told me, "I am not religious, but religion is what keeps many people from accepting my family. So it is a big issue in my life. The Pope thinks that my family is unholy. That fact alone is enough to deter me from being religious, but I have other reasons as well."

Youth with LGBTQ parents come from many religious backgrounds and have different experiences regarding faith. Many individuals who were interviewed for this book have weak connections to religion because of the discomfort they've felt; others talked about feeling more connected to spirituality than religion. For example, Sara considers herself to be "spiritual" and is still trying to better understand how religion fits into her life, if at all: "Right now, being in a college surrounded by Christians, Buddhists, Muslims, Jews, and Atheists, I am questioning my own religion. However, during my nineteen years of life, spirituality, not religion, has definitely impacted my view of my parents. My moms are very spiritual, and in times of trouble they often found peace within their own accepting spirituality. I think at times this was true for me too."

Whatever you decide, it's about being comfortable and making decisions based on your heart and your values. Sometimes religion or spiritual practices are passed down from parents, but it is also good to do some soul-searching and questioning on your own.

Unsurprisingly, the majority of individuals who reported strong connections to their faith also experienced few or no instances where they felt uncomfortable or discriminated against in their spiritual environments, whether they attended mosques, churches, synagogues, or meditation centers. This may stem from their parents having made sure that their kids were in supportive environments. There are literally hundreds of worship centers across the United States that are now accepting and affirming of LGBTQ individuals and their families.

Aaron, age twenty-eight, has parents with different religious views, but they both have made sure that their spiritual environment is a reflection of their family and core beliefs. Aaron shared, "I grew up with one mom who was Jewish, and the other was fairly agnostic. We went to a very LGBTQ-inclusive synagogue when I was growing up and so I have always connected my spirituality to social justice. Having that community be open and affirming with my family has made me embrace spirituality in a way that I think makes me lucky—not everyone finds acceptance in their spiritual communities." Although Aaron had a positive religious experience, there are still far too many religious groups that spew hateful rhetoric and intolerance for LGBTQ individuals and their families, and there's no denying that this has an effect on us.

ARE SOME RELIGIOUS GROUPS MORE OPEN TO OUR FAMILIES?

Even if a standard policy of inclusion is not present in every single religious setting, more progressive religious groups have created policies that support all people, regardless of sexual orientation. Many religious groups are peacefully standing up and speaking out against homophobia and other forms of injustice. For example, the United Church of Christ ran a TV ad that showed gays and other nontraditional worshippers being ejected from the church pews. The commercial was effective at portraying how exclusive some houses of worship can be. The overall message was that all spiritual groups should be open-armed and accessible.

LGBTQ-welcoming religious communities are definitely needed because, regardless of our progress, many people still question whether homosexuality is a sin and are conflicted about the place of LGBTQ persons in worship settings. In the 2007 award-winning documentary *A Jihad for Love*, by Parvez Sharma, many gay and lesbian Muslims expressed that they felt as if there was no space for them within Islam. In mainstream Islam, being homosexual is considered *haram* (sinful) and against *Shari'a* law (Islamic law). Furthermore, in countries where *Shari'a* law is integrated into state

I'm not religious, and I don't believe what the Torah, the Qur'an, or the Bible says. Is that okay?

Of course. Religion and/or God are very personal experiences—and some of us don't believe in those things either. You do not have to follow anyone else or their doctrine. Let your heart, mind, morals, and common sense guide your actions and beliefs.

and civil law codes, homosexuality is often punishable by jail time, physical retribution (such as lashings), or even death. There are very few organizations that support and advance the cause of LGBTQ Muslims, and one of those if Al-Fatiha.In the United States, there is only one LGBTQ-friendly mosque listed at Al-Fatiha's website, and that is Masjid Darussalam, located in the heart of San Francisco.

So even if there is a growing acceptance of homosexuality within Islam, those spaces are few and far between. However, Islam is not the only religion that has a difficult time accepting both the word of their religious doctrine and same-sex unions. The ultra-fundamentalist sects of Judaism also believe that homosexuality is unnatural and punishable by death, based on Biblical interpretations. Sadly, extremism can be found in most religions.

Religion is a tricky subject because there are dozens of sects within each religion, and those sects may hold very different views. For example, Reconstructionist, Reform, and to some extent Conservative Jews are very accepting of homosexuality and are constantly dialoguing and debating from within to accept LGBTQ individuals and their families into their folds. A portion of the Modern Orthodox stream is also slowly and cautiously beginning to grapple with the issue. This is very important. Challenging prejudice and hatred has to come from individuals within the religion—from those who love, respect, and have knowledge of that religion. If you have a problem with how your religion, or your specific place of worship, sees homosexuality, then you and your family are the best individuals to talk to other members about altering this perspective.

If we could stop talking about the anti-gay sentiments in some religious environments, we would. The reality, however, is that there is still much work to be done. In 2003, the Pew Forum on Religion and Public Life conducted a survey on religious beliefs and homosexuality.

They found these startling facts:

- Most Americans (55 percent) believe that homosexual behavior is a sin, while 33 percent disagree.
- Deeply religious people are far more likely to see homosexual behavior as sinful than are the less religious.
- Only 18 percent of non-religious respondents feel that homosexual behavior is sinful.
- The vast majority of regular churchgoers who hear about homosexuality in church say the message is a negative rather than a neutral or positive one. Overall 76 percent say their clergy discourage homosexuality, while 4 percent say clergy favor acceptance of it; only 16 percent say their clergy take no position when they speak about the issue.

HOW ARE CHILDREN OF GAYS AFFECTED BY RELIGION?

Just like everything else, religion plays a role in how we see the world. Our experiences with religion sometimes bring us closer to our faith and sometimes move us farther away. Orson, age thirty-two, who grew up with a Guyanese-Canadian gay father, says, "I am Catholic but am not practicing. I have some issues with Catholicism because of my affiliations with the gay community. I don't feel like the two sides of me are compatible. I haven't yet found a space where I can be fully who I am. I feel like Catholicism makes me put a part of who I am, or who my family is, on the doorstep before I enter."

Many of the adults with LGBTQ parents I spoke with felt similarly, and as a result, many have chosen a path of spirituality rather than organized religion. This is the case for Marie, an adopted thirty-five-year old with an African-American bisexual mother. She told me, "I'm spiritual. I didn't grow up in the church. I've been exposed to so many religions that it's hard to pick just one. Religion tends to isolate people from one another. Many churches and religions aren't accepting of homosexuality. I don't believe in that—that it's not an acceptable thing in God's eyes. He created us all. If you're born like that, how can that be wrong?"

Marie's younger sister Alissa has a less accepting view of her mother's sexuality. Alissa is twenty-nine years old and lives in Atlanta. She's Christian and attends church regularly. "Having a gay parent has shaped me," she says. "It pushed me towards religion. I read the Bible, and everyone's against homosexuality. It's not about religion. It's about everyday morals. I don't think homosexuality is right. It's wrong. It's such a hard situation, though, and it's hard to say what someone else is doing wrong. I can't judge anybody. God gives you a chance, a choice. I love everybody, but it's not all the way right." Having an LGBTQ parent can sometimes leave us feeling conflicted and at odds with our parents. In some instances, we outright reject them.

I went through a phase when I thought my mother's homosexuality was wrong, and I didn't like her as a result. I felt this way because my grandma told me being gay was bad, and my best friend's mother told me that my mom was committing a sin against God and that she would go to hell for it. The various African-American Baptist churches I attended as a child, from the deep South to the Midwest, expressed the same beliefs and viciously rallied against homosexuality from the pulpit. I heard this homophobic message over and over. This created a silent and uncomfortable rift between my mother and me. This also created a chasm between me and the African–American Baptist church. Fortunately, some of these churches are now giving a more accepting message to their congregations, reducing the isolation that many black LGBTQ families may feel.

Choosing to stand by your religious beliefs or your parent(s) can be a tough decision. However, you shouldn't ever have to choose. Our families should be just as acceptable and visible as other families in religious settings. Kerry, age sixteen, definitely feels that having a lesbian mom impacted her, but it has not made her question her faith or her mother's sexuality. "Religion has been a constant in my life, whereas my mom only came out five or six years ago. So I guess, in my case, it's a bit more a case of my mom being gay impacting my religion. I'm still a hardcore born-again

Christian. I'm just probably a lot more accepting than most. I think that it's up to God to judge what is right or wrong, and that will happen eventually. Whether or not being gay is considered 'wrong' in God's eyes should have no impact whatsoever upon how I treat people, gay or straight."

Some individuals with LGBTQ parents have been hurt by organized religion, but it's not the religion that hurts. It's ignorant people within the religion. Don't let someone stop you from embracing your faith. Find another place of worship or confront the ignorant in the name of a loving, peaceful, all-accepting God.

I argue that it's very forward-thinking to be committed to the religion of your choice and still be supportive of the LGBTQ community, regardless of your religion's stance on the issue. I surveyed several individuals from the religious community to ask their opinions about LGBTQ families and how they can support us. Susan Saxe, chief operating officer for the Alliance for Jewish Renewal, warns us against supporting the hateful "traditions" that our religions hold on to. She explains, "Rote observance of tradition and ritual is not the standard by which someone's faith should be measured. If someone tells you that their religion dictates a certain attitude or action, the question to ask is not whether tradition or text seems to support it— anyone can twist anything to support their prejudices. The real question is whether it is consistent with the golden rule of treating others as you would want to be treated *in their situation*." In essence, we need to acknowledge our bias and be willing to release judgment. Saxe also advocates that we keep at the forefront of our minds and hearts the very qualities that make us humane and just. Saxe asks, "Is it consistent with justice, fairness, compassion, kindness, generosity, and humility (not being a holier-than-thou know-it-all)? If not, then no matter what tradition or text they are using to justify their prejudices, then they, not you or your parents, are going against the most basic, fundamental tenets of their faith. They are going against the fifth commandment (honor your parents) as well as the ninth (don't go around bad-mouthing your neighbors)! They are the ones with a problem, not you or your family." And to this eloquent response, I say, "Amen, sista!" We should not continue to lug around the guilt, shame, or hatred that some bigots put on us in the name of religion. Let them carry their own baggage while you go on with your business.

Individuals with LGBTQ parents can actually move religion forward by simply being present and advocating for what's right within the walls of that religion. Wade, age twenty-nine, shares, "At first, I hated the fact that my dad was gay. I bought into the whole religious line about gays going to hell. But it was a collision between my love for my dad and my religious belief. The love won—which is also a win for religion in the long run. So basically, having a gay dad changed my religion. My spirituality now focuses much more on the value of human relationships—caring for those in pain, and embracing the richness of existence—rather than trying to live up to unlivable religious rules." Wade shows us a great example of an internal process that can happen when your religious values hit up against something that doesn't feel quite right—like not supporting our parents. In the end, it's about thinking for yourself and not compromising your values or relationships.

In Islam, there is a similar sentiment. The term *Ijtihad* stands for independent reasoning, which means that instead of following faith blindly, one should use critical thinking. The religious group and/or leader that does not want you to think for yourself is probably not the best because both are based on following a human's directions and traditions, not necessarily following God's direction—which is to love others as yourself (even if you disagree with them).

On her website, www.irshadmanji.com, Muslim activist and author Irshad Manji says that the "do unto others as you'd have them do unto you" motto is the golden rule of living—much more of a code to live by than judging others. According to Manji's website, "Prophet Muhammad himself said that religion is the way we conduct ourselves toward others. By that standard, how we Muslims behave *is* Islam." This "behavior" that Manji speaks of means that no person, in the name of religion, has the right to treat another person poorly because of differing beliefs. We still must lead with respect and work on human goals together, especially if we disagree on religion. You don't have to agree with someone else to treat them with respect.

IS HOMOSEXUALITY A SIN?

Loving someone of the same sex is not a sin. Love is never wrong. You never have to choose between your religion and your parents. God loves and accepts us all. It is humans who have a problem with acceptance, not God. There will be tough questions, but you can figure some of them out with help from God, your parents, and your spiritual community. So be at peace. Although I'm clearly stating my own stance about this, it's important to bring in some expert opinions on this question as well.

"No, homosexuality is not wrong. Judaism teaches us that we should treat other human beings with the same respect, if not more, that we hope to receive from others. Our sacred text, the Torah, teaches us that we ought to "love your neighbor as yourself" (Leviticus 19:18). This verse follows from the foundational story of Creation in the beginning of the book of Genesis that teaches that every human being is created in the image of God (Genesis 1:26–27). So, having been created in the image of God, it is our responsibility to treat others kindly and respect others, no matter what, because of the "godliness" within each of us."

—RABBI EVON YAKAR,
educational director of Temple Chai, a Member Congregation
of the Union for Reform Judaism (www.templechai.com)

"Absolutely not. Homosexuality is a God-given expression of wholeness for a great many people."

—LINDA REPPOND,
managing director of the International Youth & Family Ministries, United
Centers for Spiritual Living (www.unitedcentersforspiritualliving.org)

"No. Homosexuality is not a sin. People have been misinformed about homosexuality as it relates to the Bible. In the Christian faith, Jesus never mentioned homosexuality. As a matter of fact, homoerotic love did not exist during the times

of the Bible or in any Biblical scripture. What existed were groups of people who practiced same-sex activity without love, but for power."

—REVEREND KAREN HUTT,
a United Church of Christ member and Unitarian
Universalist and gay parent (www.uua.org)

"I think the amount of innocent homosexuals out there having endless nights of crying and praying for help are proof enough that this is a dilemma that cannot be overcome. So they need to be supported by society. And what makes it more difficult is that society is shouting out to them in a very prejudice[d] way: 'I cannot accept you because you are not like me.'"

—MUHSIN HENDRICKS,
imam, Islamic scholar, gay parent, and founder of Al-Fitrah, the
first queer Muslim organization in South Africa, which is now
known as the Inner Circle (http://theinnercircle.org.za)

Today, there are more places of worship that are accepting of LGBTQ families than ever before. Popular websites, such as gaychurch.org and soulforce.org, list safe, welcoming places of worship by state, making it easier for LGBTQ families to find positive centers of worship and to be fully who they are. In *50 Ways to Support Lesbian and & Gay Equality*, Reverend Dr. Troy Perry writes, "Increasingly, LGBTQ people are reclaiming our spirituality. No one else can define us or limit us. We've reclaimed the positive, hope-filled message of our faith and worked to liberate it from the biases and prejudices that too many religious leaders imposed on it." Because LGBTQ parents are reclaiming their faith and speaking out against injustice, we reap the benefits of healthier spiritual environments.

None of us should have to feel rejection or disdain for something that was meant to bring us closer to God. If no particular religious outlet works for you, develop your own spiritual beliefs. How (or if) you choose to worship is between you and God. Each of us has our own personal relationship with God, which no religion or person can come between. When times get tough, let your faith or personal beliefs guide you through. Try not to let negative people or experiences pull you away from God and your faith. It is in those times that you get stronger and develop your value system and core beliefs. It is in those times that you can do God's work of bringing humanity together in love, peace, understanding, and mutual respect.

OUR**VOICES**

HOW HAS RELIGION IMPACTED YOUNG PEOPLE WITH LGBTQ PARENTS?

"I was very religious for quite some time, and I actually remember beginning to question my parents, thinking they might be doing something wrong. I'm not a strong Christian at the moment, but for a while, I was quite confused."

—LORNE, 15

"Religion hasn't had much of an impact on my views of having LGBTQ parents. Other religious views of LGBTQ people have made me angry and defiant, but my love for my parents has never changed. When I hear other people talking about their religion-biased views on LGBTQ people and families, I try to make sure they know how wrong they can be at times. Religions that don't support the LGBTQ community make it harder for those who support families and people because they preach hate to people when love is what they need to hear."

—EMILY, 16

"We go to Metropolitan Community Church Illiana, where almost all of the members are gay. It doesn't matter if you're gay or not. Just be who you are and follow your heart."

—ASHLEE, 12

"I am Christian, and I know Christians that are homosexual. I do believe homosexuality is a sin. However, I don't think that it should be. I think gays should have the freedom to like whom they like."

—CHRIS, 15

"I was not raised religious, though my extended family is religious. Fortunately, I have never been in a community where the religious influence was so strong and discriminatory that I felt directly impacted by it. Though on a national scale, I am in disbelief that with all of the United States' so called 'civil rights,' gay people don't have the right to simple things like marriage."

—CARMEN LEAH, 22

"I believe in God, but not in the Catholic church that I belong to. I truly believe that God has blessed me by giving me two loving parents. The fact that my parents are gay is beside the point. They are my parents and they love me. There are others in the world that have less than that, and I thank God every time I go home and see them show affection towards each other and towards me. A loving family is the best of God's gifts to me."

—SCOUT, 21

"My family is not religious. I have heard my fair share of anti-gay religious views, but I feel that I have plenty of comebacks to any comments and am willing to argue my point with any religious person who challenges me. I don't believe that either they or [I] are right and the other is wrong, but at the same time, I will fight for what I believe in. Because of the often negative opinions about gay families in religion, I have become wary of religious organizations and do sometimes find myself prejudiced against anyone religious."

—HANNAH, 19

THE**EXPERT'S**JOURNAL**PAGES**

SOURCES

Pew Research Center for the People and the Press, "Religious Beliefs Underpin Opposition to Homosexuality," November 2003.

Muhsin Hendricks, Voice of the Cape Radio Debate, www.mask.org.za/article.php?cat=islam&id=729 (June 20, 2005).

Troy Perry, "Keep the Faith," in *50 Ways to Support Lesbian & Gay Equality,* eds. Meredith Maran and Angela Watrous, 124–125 (Maui: Inner Ocean Publishing, 2005).

Chapter Seven

Activism 101

"Words mean nothing. Action is the only thing. Doing. That's the only thing."
—Earnest Gaines

I had never even heard of COLAGE **until 2000,** when I happened to be chatting with a friend of mine who was a gay parent. She wanted me to get involved in an LGBTQ family conference she was planning and connected me with the phenomenal people at COLAGE. I was in my twenties and felt pretty comfortable relating to the kids, especially since I too had grown up with a gay parent. So I ended up facilitating some sessions with the kids of gay parents who were attending the conference. It was exhilarating to work with those teens, and I was on a natural high for days afterwards. Then I got angry. Why wasn't there a COLAGE or any other group around when I was young? I could have used that type of support when I was being teased.

But then another, more important thought came to me. Why wasn't there an organization specifically for youth with LGBTQ parents in Chicago, the third-largest city in the nation, at that point in time? I knew there had to be tons of youngsters in Chicago just like me, thinking that they were the only kids in the city with a gay parent. At that time, Chicago had a huge LGBTQ population and many progressive LGBTQ organizations (and they still do!), but none that were specifically for children with an LGBTQ parent.

I decided I needed to do something about this, and so I turned my initial angry response into a call for action. With the help of COLAGE, I started the first Chicago COLAGE chapter that very same year—and the result of everything I've learned over the past decade turned into the book that you are now reading. However, it would not have happened if I hadn't surrounded myself with others (within COLAGE) who also had LGBTQ parents. I felt a sense of community and gained different perspectives about a variety of issues pertaining to our families. These friends supported me every step of the way—to create the chapter, to write the book, and to be visible and help others be visible too. This is one reason why it's so important to reach out to COLAGE or organizations like it. It only makes your personal efforts stronger and keeps you connected to people with similar experiences and familial backgrounds.

My parent is always dragging me to all of these LGBTQ-centered events and it's getting on my nerves. What should I do?

Nicely tell you parent(s) to lay off. Remember, it's not what you say, it's how you say it. Try, "Dear parent, you have always taught me to be an individual and to communicate my needs. As much as I respect LGBTQ rights and your attempt to make sure I have the best, I am an individual, needing my own space. I hope that you can respect that I don't want to attend all of your events. It is not a slight to you, I just have my own interests, such as . . . " This should do the trick. If not, you can always stage a protest, complete with banners saying, "Hell no, I won't go!" At least you all will get a chuckle out of the situation.

If you are gungho about equal rights and advocating for LGBTQ families, this beginner's activism section is for you. Sometimes the term "activism" makes people think about taking to the streets and being really active in politics—and that can be a turnoff. But activism is much broader than doing sit-ins or having to put yourself in a place you would rather not be. The truth is that everything we do is political. The way you dress is a political statement. Many of the views you hold are political (like your thoughts on when teens should be allowed to drive, or whether your parents should be allowed to legally marry). Making the decision to read this book can be perceived as a political action. And all of it has an impact on you and the larger society.

Basically, politics dictate who gets a say in the way we live, act, and breathe. Becoming a leader is about developing ideas on a certain topic, creating a plan, getting others on board, and turning that belief into a policy, an activity, or a way of life.

Your local school council helps decide what issues are relevant at your school and how to make it a better learning environment. Your student government determines what the needs and interests of the students are, and they take them to the school officials to see if policies can be changed to address student concerns. It's all political, and we can choose to be active in those politics.

Activism has been defined in many ways, including "the practice based on direct action to effect changes in social conditions, government, etc." Okay, that's the definition we want. In a nutshell, activism is what you do to make the world a better place. Maybe you notice that there's a lot of trash at the local park and you organize a group of friends to do something about it. This is being an activist. Maybe you're sick and tired of the girls sitting on the bench during coed football or soccer games and decide to create an all-girls team, or find an adult who will support your idea. Welcome to the world of activism. The key to activism is to act on your beliefs.

Why would anyone want to be an activist? There are many reasons, but the main one is because you're a person who thinks finding solutions to problems is more fulfilling than sitting around complaining about what is wrong with the world.

TOP 10 REASONS TO BE A YOUTH ACTIVIST

10. Because it's an easy way to rack up those mandatory service learning hours.

9. Because you suck at sports.

8. Because you're getting tired of watching reality show reruns.

7. Because you want to outshine your goody-two-shoes sibling.

6. Because you will make your parents proud (which may get you an allowance increase or that new iPod you've been wanting).

5. Because being an activist sounds way cooler than being a cheerleader or a jock. (Admit it, being an activist sounds gangsta.)

4. Because you get to be obnoxiously opinionated about your beliefs.

3. Because you get to piss off people and do something positive at the same time.

2. Because you care about social justice and a whole bunch of other righteous stuff.

1. Because you were born to make a mark on this world.

Now that I've convinced you of all the great reasons to get active, let's see what an activist actually does. Activists are people who are passionate enough (read: angry enough) about an issue that they are willing to get off their butts and do something about it. You can be an activist for creating tastier cafeteria meals, bringing the arts back into your school, and fighting neighborhood crime. You first need to decide what issues are important to you. It isn't just about fighting for LGBTQ family rights, although that's *muy importante*; it's about speaking out for the things you believe in.

I'm a strong believer, although I'm partial, that children with LGBTQ parents are among the most open-minded, caring individuals in the universe and are instrumental in making this world a better place. In part, it is because we know how it feels to be discriminated against, which tends to make us more empathetic toward others and other people's issues. And I'm not the only one who thinks so. Many of the teens and young adults that I interviewed felt that they were heavily influenced by their parents to advocate for what is right. How do you think organizations like COLAGE, the NAACP (National Association for the Advancement of Colored People), and NOW (National Organization for Women) got started? People got tired of being crapped on, and even more tired of not having their needs addressed. Instead of moping around, however, they said, "Let's start our own organization and fight for the things that matter to us!"

We can all contribute to the greater good in our own little way. When thinking about how you can make the world a better place, there are several important questions that you need to answer in order to get your ideas out of your head and into the universe.

- What are the top social issues that are important to me?
- How did I become interested in this?
- How can I help to make these situations better?
- What challenges might I face?
- How can I work around these challenges?
- What friends, allies, or organizations can help me to make my activism goals a reality?
- What am I currently involved in that makes the world a better place?

If you aren't really active but would like to become more involved, check out this next exercise to help you on your journey into activism. Circle the areas that you would love to get involved in to make the world a better place. Add your own causes, if necessary.

Animal Rights	Healthcare Reform	Poverty
Assisting the Elderly	Helping Children	Prison Reform
Civil Rights	HIV/AIDS Advocacy	Racial Equality
Disability Rights	Housing Reform	Rape Victim Advocate
Domestic Violence	Hunger	Reproductive Rights
Drug Prevention	Immigration Issues	Sexual Abuse
Drunk Driving	LGBTQ Family Rights	Size Discrimination
Education Reform	LGBTQ Rights	Supporting Senior Citizens
Environmental Issues	Literacy	Unemployment
Gender Equality	Mental Illness	Voting
Gun Control	Physical Abuse	Women's Rights

_____   _____   _____
_____   _____   _____
_____   _____   _____
_____   _____   _____
_____   _____   _____

After answering these questions and taking stock of the causes you care about, it is important to educate yourself about the things you circled. There are several sides to every problem, and the more knowledge you have, the better you'll be able to come up with sound solutions. Many issues are interconnected, so you may find yourself entrenched in several struggles at once. For example, your main activism interest may be helping to keep children safe from gang violence. However, this will mean you'll find out about other challenges related to gang violence, such as poverty, oppression, racism, gun control laws, drug trafficking, street politics, and interracial tensions. Being well-educated on a social justice issue helps temper some of the emotion and snap judgment (which may be well-meaning, but nonetheless, counterproductive to your efforts), and helps you understand where others are coming from, even if their perspective is different from yours.

25 FUN THINGS YOU CAN DO TO KICK OFF YOUR ACTIVISM

- Clean up your neighborhood
- Rake leaves for each elderly person on your block
- Give to the homeless
- Become an advocate for the under-represented rape victims
- Coordinate a gift drive
- Donate some of your savings to your favorite charity or cause
- Donate gently used clothes
- Offer to paint someone's church, home, school, etc.
- Volunteer in your neighborhood
- Host a talent show and donate the proceeds
- Donate children's books

- Write/direct a play and donate the proceeds
- Give blood
- Sponsor a letter-writing campaign for US troops
- Help at a shelter
- Respond to an issue in your local newspaper
- Host a poetry slam
- Write to your congressperson and VOTE if you're 18+
- Wash cars for a cause
- Host a bake sale and donate the proceeds
- Practice random acts of kindness
- Speak out against injustice at a rally
- Start a Gay–Straight Alliance at your school or a COLAGE chapter in your city/town/region

QUICK TIPS

1. **Make sure you don't overextend yourself.** You can't help others if you aren't taking care of yourself first. Make sure you are rested and that your school and personal life are in order (not perfect, just going strong) before you take on the world.
2. **Be a leader, not a follower.** You have to figure out what makes you tick and (whether others are on board or not) stand up for what you believe. Don't be afraid. Stand up and speak up. At the same time, know that there are hundreds of different ways to be a leader. You don't have to be interested in speaking to a crowd of millions. You just need to have ideas and the passion to make them happen. You can lead by example, and even shy people can be leaders.
3. **Talk is cheap.** Don't waste time just gabbing about a societal problem (unless you want to be a political science professor). Create a plan, get support, make time, and do it!

OUR**VOICES**

HOW ARE YOU INVOLVED IN YOUR COMMUNITY
AND WHAT IS THE SOURCE OF YOUR ACTIVISM?

"Involvement in my community is one of my highest priorities. I love to be involved in as many community summits as possible. Besides participating in the LGBTQ Center of Utah events, I enjoy volunteering for many other organizations. I feel it is rewarding when I am able to help others. It makes my life fulfilling. Part of the reason I am so passionate is I have grown up in a diverse family, in which I have been open to more ideas. I have seen others put up huge walls and not see the importance of diversity. Watching closed-minded people is infuriating, but it motivates me to try and make a difference, and to help people see things from a different perspective. I wish others could see that uniqueness does not make them a bad person. I do the best that I can to help others see this. If I am able to influence even one person in the slightest way, that makes a difference. Volunteering and being active in my community helps me and others continue to grow, and together we can keep striving to make the world a better place."

—CARA, 16

"I am involved with local women's organizations, COLAGE, and the upstart of the local Queer Community Center. I publish a zine called Wobbly Little Legs, write blogs, and speak locally on the subject of queer family rights and marriage equality."

—CHELSIA, 28

"When I was in high school, I testified before the North Dakota State Legislature on a safe schools bill that would have added sexual orientation to the list of identities [protected] from harassment and bullying. It didn't pass, but it was a great opportunity. I was also heavily involved in many press conferences and interviews, especially when the ND Family Alliance was petitioning for an ND Marriage Amendment. My moms and I helped form a group called "Decline to Sign," and we protested at many events. I also helped my moms start the first ever Bismarck-Mandan Pride Fest,

which was a lot of fun, and it is still continuing to this day. And I guess you could say that my activism interests come not only from all of the oppression my family and I have [experienced], but also from all of the oppression my numerous LGBTQ friends have [experienced]. If their children won't help them, who will?"

—SARA, 19

"I volunteer at Pride and always walk in the AIDS Walk. I find that Pride is a great experience, and I'm always pleased to be completely involved in my community. Although I'm straight, I truly feel that my community is the LGBTQ community. They all accept me for who I am and what I believe, and I show them the same respect and love. I started becoming active in the community when I opened my eyes and saw the blatant civil rights violations occurring within this country towards the LGBTQ community. I reasoned that if I, a 'straight person,' were to become actively involved in this cause, then it might prove to change some people's minds about things like same-sex marriage and gay adoption."

—SCOUT, 21

"When my dad started her transition, I realized that there was room to be more open-minded and accepting of difference. This was a valuable lesson, because we can always work to be more accepting and consider other important issues. If my dad hadn't transitioned, I may not have considered transgender rights, but now I consider them a priority in the activist work that I do and will continue to undertake throughout my lifetime. I am very invested in the queerspawn movement and have a deep desire to provide resources and support to other children of transgendered parents."

—MONICA, 26

ON**MARRIAGE**AND**DISCRIMINATION**
by Cleopatra Bezis, 15

Red, White, and Blue.
Many people say that these colors don't run.
Then why am I running from them?
Do you not see, what hatred they possess?
Love is not blind
It is invisible.
But love has the power
To be exuberating, exhilarating, exciting, expressive, and empowering.
How can colors demolish that?
What do they stand for?
To me, they stand for hate, power, discrimination,
racism, greed, anger, and control.
What do they mean to you?
For colors are just colors, that's what you think.
Then why do you respect them, worship them, believe in them,
And trust them to make us a better nation?
People have rights and our anger will not subside until those colors run.
For the true colors, which stand for love, respect, dignity, and equality will not run,
And this hatred that we have embodied will subside.
Those being discriminated against will
Finally be able to show
Their true colors
FREELY

This poem was first published in *Focus on MY Family: A Queerspawn Anthology*, created by the COLAGE Youth Leadership and Action Program.

THE**EXPERT'S**JOURNAL**PAGES**

SOURCES

Webster's II New Riverside Dictionary, Office ed., n. "activism"

Scott Beale and Abeer Abdalla, *Millennial Manifesto* (Instant Publisher, 2003).

Conclusion

This book is about self-empowerment because we have to feel empowered before we can effect change and make our world a better place.

There are lots of ways to experience change. Effecting change, for instance, is different than embracing change. And although change can be good, it can also be scary. Fear tends to be an enemy of change. Fear can stop us from wanting things to change, and so part of getting to the next step is to have strategies for overcoming our fears. Try to think of something you've done that's felt really scary. Mostly this involves doing things on your own for the first time. Maybe it was the first time you ever flew by yourself or the first time you spoke in front of a crowd. Maybe it was the first time you told a friend that you had an LGBTQ parent. Whatever it was, take a moment to recall the feeling of fear. The anxiety, or the butterflies, or whatever feeling bubbles up for you usually arises because you're doing something that has an unknown outcome. When you fly with your parents, it's not scary because they know what to do. But when you tackle something all by yourself, you need to do it a few times before you really get comfortable with it. Well, it's the same when you take a stand for what you believe in. At first it will probably be really scary, but over time it'll feel like second nature.

The self-discovery activities in this book are designed to help you feel more brave, supported, and knowledgeable. So now that you're nearing the end of the book, take some time to go back to some of the exercises you might have skipped. Consider filling out all the journal pages with your thoughts, and take this time to consider how you want to make an impact. With your insight, your story, and your passion, you're a fighting machine, ready to demand social justice for all people regardless of race, sexual orientation, class, ability, or gender.

It's important to note here that there are many family types out there, and I realize that not every type of family got equal attention in this book. But no matter what your family looks like, you are as important to our struggle as the next person. If you've felt your experience was not adequately covered by this book, that's all the more reason to be vocal about your own experience. I've been encouraging each of you to find avenues for self-expression and talking about your experiences in a safe environment. I hope this book can offer you a first step. Whether we have a parent living with HIV or come from a family where one parent is transgender, each of us has a powerful personal story that makes us the unique people we are.

I encourage each and every one of you to embrace the diversity of our community and to be aware of all of the ways our families may intersect. Some of you may live in rural areas or outside of the United States. Some of your parents are married, while others are still fighting for their rights, and others of us still have single parents, some of whom have never been married. Some of us have parents who wouldn't get married if you paid them (my mom being one of them). Some of us feel at home in queer space, and some of us would never think of attending an LGBTQ conference. We are warriors, thinkers, and humanitarians. We are intuitive, visionary, and leaders of the future. We are who our experiences have made us. We, and our families, are ever-changing—and hopefully for the better.

We are warrior spirits making our way on this journey called life. We are tilling our own soil and will not be defined by anyone but us. We will claim our truth and make no apologies for who we are and from whence we came. We will only fight the fights we feel are worth fighting, even if that doesn't include the fights society expects. We will remember to love. We will evolve. We will blaze a new trail for others to follow. And always, we will be individuals with LGBTQ parents, no less and so much more.

Thank you for taking the time to read and fully engage in this book. We hope *Let's Get This Straight* has helped you to feel empowered and made you laugh and feel connected to a diverse and loving community. We are also optimistic that it might even spark rich dialogue in your family, your community, and among your peers. We look forward to receiving your feedback, which can be directed to Tina Fakhrid-Deen at tina@tinatfakhriddeen.com.

YOUR TURN

What have you discovered about yourself from reading this book?

_____

_____

_____

_____

_____

_____

_____

_____

_____

_____

_____

_____

_____

_____

_____

_____

_____

_____

_____

_____

_____

_____

What is your personal truth?

_____

_____

_____

_____

_____

_____

_____

_____

_____

_____

_____

_____

_____

_____

_____

_____

_____

_____

_____

_____

_____

_____

_____

In what small ways can you fight homophobia?

_____

_____

_____

_____

_____

_____

_____

_____

_____

_____

_____

_____

_____

_____

_____

_____

_____

_____

_____

_____

_____

In honor of all that you are, list all of your titles that span beyond having an LGBTQ parent (i.e., writer, student, spiritualist, cyclist, parent, french fry goddess, etc.).

_____

_____

_____

_____

_____

_____

_____

_____

_____

_____

_____

_____

_____

_____

_____

_____

_____

_____

_____

How has reading *Let's Get This Straight* helped you on your journey (if at all)?

_____

_____

_____

_____

_____

_____

_____

_____

_____

_____

_____

_____

_____

_____

_____

_____

_____

_____

_____

_____

_____

_____

_____

_____

Fun Corner

25 Comebacks to Clueless Questions

"Now remember, there are no stupid questions, only stupid people."
—Mr. Garrison on *South Park*

People say the dumbest things about our families, and it's time to strike back. Here are twenty-five deliciously smart comebacks to combat stupid questions and dumb comments. So often, we are hit with crazy comments and we sit stunned, unable to respond. Usually, it is days later when we think of a perfectly witty thing to say, but by then, of course, the offender is always long gone. These comebacks were compiled by the dozens of individuals who were surveyed for this book and are meant to empower you and jog your memory the next time some knucklehead slips up and rubs you the wrong way.

1. **Clueless Question:** How did you get here if you have two moms?
   Clever Response: I got here from a sperm and an egg just like everyone else. How I got here and who my family is are two different things.

2. **Clueless Question:** What do you call your two dads?
   Clever Response: My parents.

3. **Clueless Question:** If your parents are gay, does that mean you're gay too?
   Clever Response: With your logic, my parents should be straight since their parents were probably straight. Therefore, it's an illogical question.

4. **Clueless Question:** Do your parents ever try to make you gay?
   Clever Response: It's too late.

5. **Clueless Question:** Have you ever seen your parents have sex?
   Clever Response: Ewww. Have you seen your parents have sex?

6. **Clueless Question:** Do you think gays should be able to adopt children?
   Clever Response: It would depend on whether they're good parents or not.

7. **Clueless Question:** How do kids of gays turn out?
   Clever Response: In need of therapy, like everyone else.

8. **Ignorant Comment:** That's so gay.
   Clever Response: Yes, that was fabulous, wasn't it?

9. **Ignorant Comment:** Gays shouldn't be allowed to marry.
   Clever Response: Neither should idiots, so I guess you'll be single for the rest of your life.

10. **Ignorant Comment:** I think gays are gross.
    Clever Response: They can't be any more gross than that huge booger in your nose. (Then walk away.)

11. **Clueless Question:** So if your mom's a lesbian, does that mean she, like, hits on you?
    Clever Response: Yeah, of course. Doesn't your straight dad hit on you?

12. **Clueless Question:** Do you think that your dad will come on to me if I am alone in the room with him?
    Clever Response: I doubt it. He's gay, not a pedophile. Do you know the difference?

13. **Clueless Question:** Are your parents really lesbians?
    Clever Response: No, they just like the attention.

14. **Clueless Question:** Which one is your real mom?
    Clever Response: Since they both respond to "mom," I suspect they both are.

15. **Clueless Question:** Do your parents sleep in the same bed?
    Clever Response: No, one of them sleeps on the kitchen table. Breakfast can be a real pain.

16. **Clueless Question:** Since your dad is gay, do you all do really gay stuff?
    Clever Response: Of course. We went to see Barbara Streisand last night.

17. **Clueless Question:** Who is that other guy with your dad?
    Clever Response: His parole officer.

18. **Clueless Question:** Don't you think your parent being gay is a sin?
    Clever Response: No. If it is, it can't be any worse than the one you're committing by judging others. So get off my back.

19. **Ignorant Comment:** Your family isn't a real family.
    Clever Response: Who died and made you the family police?

20. **Clueless Question:** If you don't have a father figure in the house, how will you learn to be a man?
    Clever Response: By watching ESPN like every other guy, especially since my mom forbids me to talk to any of my male relatives or friends of the family.

21. **Ignorant Comment:** Don't be such a fag.
    Clever Response: How does a cigarette act?

22. **Clueless Question:** Why is your dad gay?
    Clever Response: Because that's how God made him. If you don't like it, go talk to God, not me.

23. **Ignorant Comment:** Your parents are going to go to hell for being gay.
    Clever Response: They're already in hell dealing with people like you.

24. **Clueless Question:** Why do you care so much about gay stuff? Are you gay?
    Clever Response: I didn't realize one had to be gay in order to care about equality and treat people with dignity.

25. **Clever All-Purpose Response:** You know what's so gay? My family!

For additional support on responding to commonly asked questions and to support your personal activism, go to the COLAGE website and request a copy of *Speak Up. Speak Out! An Activism Guide for Youth and Adults with LGBTQ Parents*.

Additional Resources for
Youth and Young Adults

I have selected resources that I think teens with LGBTQ parents may find interesting. This is not an exhaustive list. There are many more resources available, but this is a start to improving the resources in your home, school, and local library. The COLAGE Web site also features hundreds of resources for our families.

FICTION BOOKS FOR YOUTH AND YOUNG ADULTS

Bauer, Marion Dane, ed. *Am I Blue? Coming Out from the Silence* (New York: Harper-Collins, 1995).

Bechard, Margaret. *If It Doesn't Kill You* (New York: Viking, 1999).

Block, Francesca Lia. *Girl Goddess #9: Nine Stories* (New York: HarperCollins, 1998).

Cart, Michael, ed. *Necessary Noise: Stories About Our Families as They Really Are* (New York: HarperTeen, 2003).

Durbin, Margaret. *And Featuring Bailey Wellcom as the Biscuit* (Port Orchard, WA: Windstorm Creative, 1999).

Garden, Nancy. *Annie on My Mind* (New York: Farrar, Straus, and Giroux, 1992).

——. *Holly's Secret* (New York: Farrar, Straus, and Giroux, 2000).

Garsee, Jeannine. *Say the Word* (New York: Bloomsbury USA, 2009).

Going, K.L. *King of the Screwups* (New York: Harcourt, 2009).

Goodman, Alison. *Singing the Dogstar Blues* (New York: Viking, 2003).

Halpin, Brendan. *Donorboy* (New York: Random House, 2004).

Homes, A.M. *Jack* (New York: Vintage, 1989).

Ketchum, Liza. *Newsgirl* (New York: Viking, 2009).

Myracle, Lauren. *Luv Ya Bunches* (New York: Amulet, 2009).

Peters, Julie Anne. *Luna* (New York: Megan Tingley Books, 2004).

———. *Between Mom and Jo* (New York: Megan Tingley Books, 2006).

Warren, Patricia Nell. *Billy's Boy* (Beverly Hills: Wildcat Press, 1998).

Woodson, Jacqueline. *From the Notebooks of Melanin Sun* (New York: Scholastic, 1995).

———. *House You Pass on the Way* (New York: Penguin, 2003).

NONFICTION BOOKS FOR YOUTH AND YOUNG ADULTS

Bass, Ellen, and Kate Kaufman. *Free Your Mind: The Book for Gay, Lesbian and Bisexual Youth and Their Allies* (New York: HarperCollins, 1996).

Boenke, Mary, ed. *Trans Forming Families: Real Stories About Transgendered Loved Ones* (New Castle, DE: Oak Knoll Press, 2003).

COLAGE Youth Leadership and Action Program. *Focus on MY Family: A Queerspawn Anthology* (San Francisco: COLAGE, 2004).

Epstein, Rachel. *Who's Your Daddy? And Other Writings on Queer Parenting* (Toronto: Sumach, 2009.)

Garner, Abigail. *Families Like Mine: Children of Gay Parents Tell It Like It Is* (New York: HarperCollins, 2004).

Hart, Melissa. *Gringa: A Contradictory Girlhood* (Berkeley, CA: Seal Press, 2009).

———. *The Assault of Laughter: A Daughter's Journey Back to Her Lesbian Mother* (Port Orchard, WA: Windstorm Creative, 2005).

Howey, Noelle. *Dress Codes: Of Three Girlhoods—My Mother's, My Father's, and Mine* (New York: St. Martin's Press, 2002.

Howey, Noelle, and Ellen Samuels, eds. *Out of the Ordinary: Essays on Growing Up with Gay, Lesbian, and Transgender Parents* (New York: St. Martin's Press, 2000).

Johnson, Troy. *Family Outing: What Happened When I Found Out My Mother Was Gay* (New York: Arcade, 2008).

Maran, Meredith, and Angela Watrous. *50 Ways to Support Lesbian and Gay Equality* (Novato, CA: New World Library, 2005).

Siegel, Laura, and Nancy Lamkin Olson, eds. *Out of the Closet Into Our Hearts: Celebrating Our Gay/Lesbian Family Members* (San Francisco: Leyland Publications, 2001).

Simon, Rita J., and Rhonda Roorda, eds. *In Their Own Voices: Transracial Adoptees Tell Their Stories* (New York: Columbia University Press, 2000).

Snow, Judith E. *How It Feels to Have a Gay or Lesbian Parent: A Book by Kids for Kids of All Ages* (San Francisco: Harrington Park Press, 2004).

FILMS FEATURING YOUTH WITH LGBTQ PARENTS

All God's Children. Dirs. Dee Mosbacher, Frances Reid, and Dr. Sylvia Rhue, 1996. (www.woman-vision.org)

American Primitive. Dir. Gwen Wynne, 2008. (www.americanprimitivemovie.com)

Daddy and Papa. Dir. Johnny Symons, 2002. (www.daddyandpapa.com)

In My Shoes: Stories of Youth with LGBTQ Parents. Dir. Jen Gilomen, 2005. (www.colage.org/inmyshoes/)

It's Elementary: Talking About Gay Issues in School. Dir. Debra Chasnoff, 1996. (www.womedia.org)

It's Still Elementary: Talking About Gay Issues in School. Dir. Debra Chasnoff, 2008. (www.groundspark.org)

No Dumb Questions. Dir. Melissa Regan, 2001. (www.nodumbquestions.com)

Off and Running. Dir. Nicole Opper, 2009. (www. offandrunningthefilm.com)

Our House: A Very Real Documentary About Kids of Gay and Lesbian Parents. Dir. Meema Spadola, 1999. (www.colage.org/documentary)

That's a Family! A Film for Kids About Family Diversity. Dir. Debra Chasnoff, 2000. (www.womedia.org)

Tru Loved. Dir. Stewart Wade, 2008. (www.truloved.com)

NATIONAL ORGANIZATIONS

LIFESPAN COUNSELING
Orson Morrison | www.oakparktherapists.com | www.orsonmorrison.com

COLAGE
National Office
1550 Bryant Street, Suite 830 | San Francisco, CA 94103
415/861-5437 | www.colage.org

FAMILY EQUALITY COUNCIL
PO Box 206 | Boston, MA 02133
617/502-8700 | www.familyequalitycouncil.org

NATIONAL CENTER FOR TRANSGENDER EQUALITY
Mara Keisling, Executive Director
202/903-0112 | mkeisling@nctequality.org | www.nctequality.org

PFLAG (PARENTS, FAMILIES & FRIENDS OF LESBIANS AND GAYS)
National Office
1726 M Street, NW, Suite 400 | Washington, D.C. 20036
202/467-8180 | www.pflag.org

SUMMER CAMPS FOR YOUTH WITH LGBTQ PARENTS

CAMP TEN OAKS
104 Ontario St. | Ottawa, Ontario (Canada) | K1K 1K9
613/742-5944 | www.camptenoaks.org

CAMP TEN TREES
1122 E. Pike St., PMB #1488 | Seattle, WA 98122-1488
206/985-2864 | www.camptentrees.org

FAMILY PRIDE CAMPING ASSOCIATION
Suite 121-3045 Robie Street | Halifax, Nova Scotia (Canada) | B3K 4P6
(888) 344-FPCA (toll free) | www.fpca.ca

MOUNTAIN MEADOW SUMMER CAMP
1315 Spruce Street, Suite 411 | Philadelphia, PA 19107
215/772-1107 | www.mountainmeadow.org

YOUTH ACTIVISM RESOURCES

ACLU (AMERICAN CIVIL LIBERTIES UNION)
125 Broad Street, 18th Floor | New York, NY 10004
www.aclu.org

GLAAD (GAY & LESBIAN ALLIANCE AGAINST DEFAMATION)
248 West 35th Street, 8th Floor | New York, NY 10001
212/629-3322 | www.glaad.org

HRC (HUMAN RIGHTS CAMPAIGN)
1640 Rhode Island Avenue NW | Washington, DC 20036-3278
800/777-4723 (toll free) | www.hrc.org

LAMBDA LEGAL
National Headquarters
120 Wall Street, Suite 1500 | New York, NY 10005-3904
212/809-8585 | www.lambdalegal.org

SCHOOL RESOURCES

GAY–STRAIGHT ALLIANCE NETWORK
1550 Bryant St., Suite 800 | San Francisco, CA 94103
415/552-4229 | www.gsanetwork.org

GLSEN (GAY, LESBIAN AND STRAIGHT EDUCATION NETWORK)
National Headquarters
90 Broad Street 2nd Floor | New York, NY 10004
212/727-0135 | www.glsen.org

SAFE SCHOOLS COALITION
Public Health—Seattle & King County
MS: NTH-PH-0100 | 10501 Meridian Ave. N. | Seattle, WA 98133
206/632-0662, ext. 49 | www.safeschoolscoalition.org

OTHER ONLINE RESOURCES

DONOR-CONCEIVED YOUTH
(Yahoo! group created by COLAGEr Sacha to provide additional support for donor-conceived youth)
http://groups.yahoo.com/group/donorconceivedyouth

FAMILIES LIKE MINE
(online site for individuals with LGBTQ parents created by Abigail Garner)
www.familieslikemine.org

LIFESPAN COUNSELING
Orson Morrison | www.oakparktherapists.com | www.orsonmorrison.com

QUEERSPAWN DIARIES
(online audio documentary by and about people with LGBTQ parents)
www.queerspawn.org

RAINBOW RUMPUS
(online magazine for kids with LGBTQ parents)
www.rainbowrumpus.org

SOUTHERN POVERTY LAW CENTER
www.tolerance.org

RESOURCES FOR LGBTIQ MUSLIMS AND ALLIES (WEB SITE OF MUSLIM RESOURCES AROUND THE WORLD)
www.starjack.com./qmr.html

TWO LIVES PUBLISHING (WEB SITE WITH THOROUGH RESOURCES FOR LGBTQ FAMILIES)
www.twolives.com

INCLUSIVE RELIGIOUS/SPIRITUAL WEBSITES

AL-FATIHA FOUNDATION
www.al-fatiha.org

ALEPH: ALLIANCE FOR JEWISH RENEWAL
(This is not a denomination. They are a progressive, grassroots spiritual organization.)
www.aleph.org/locate.htm

DIGNITY USA GAY, LESBIAN, BISEXUAL AND TRANSGENDER CATHOLICS
www.dignityusa.org

IMAAN—LGBT MUSLIM SUPPORT GROUP
www.imaan.org.uk

METROPOLITAN COMMUNITY CHURCH
www.mccchurch.org

QUAKER (RELIGIOUS SOCIETY OF FRIENDS)
Friends for Lesbian, Gay, Bisexual, Transgender, and Queer Concerns
www.fLGBTQqc.quaker.org

SOULFORCE
www.soulforce.org

UNITARIAN UNIVERSALISM
www.uua.org

UNITED CHURCH OF RELIGIOUS SCIENCE
www.religiousscience.org

WORLD CONGRESS OF GAY, LESBIAN, BISEXUAL JEWISH ORGANIZATIONS
www.glbtjews.org

LIFELINE (WEB) RESOURCES FOR YOUTH WITH TROUBLED PARENTS

AL-ANON, ALTEEN
(A group that helps family members of alcoholics and addicts. There is also Nar-Anon for family members of drug addicts.)
www.al-anon.alateen.org/english.html
http://nar-anon.org/index.html

CHILDHELP
(A national organization that provides support for victims of child abuse and neglect)
www.childhelp.org | 1-800-4-A-CHILD (24-hour hotline)

NATIONAL ASSOCIATION FOR CHILDREN OF ALCOHOLICS
www.nacoa.org

NATIONAL COALITION OF ANTI-VIOLENCE PROGRAMS
(Their Web site has a directory of locally-based programs that address violence, including domestic violence in the LGBTQ community.)
www.ncavp.org

COLLEGE SCHOLARSHIPS FOR STUDENTS
WITH LGBTQ PARENTS AND LGBTQ STUDENTS

COLAGE LEE DUBIN MEMORIAL SCHOLARSHIP
(for college students with LGBTQ parents)
www.colage.org

THE POINT FOUNDATION (FOR LGBTQ COLLEGE STUDENTS)
(There is also an mtvU Point Scholarship that non-LGBTQ students can apply for.)
P.O. Box 11210 | Chicago, IL 60611
866/337-6468
www.thepointfoundation.org

Acknowledgments

Thank you to all of the wonderful, brave, and trusting individuals who gave their hearts and minds to benefit this project. Your insightful and honest interviews, surveys, and emails have grounded, motivated, and humbled me. Thank you for allowing me to share part of your story with the world. I am indebted to you. This book is ours, written by our collective voices, experiences, and spirits. Ashe!

I want to thank and bow to all of the parents who allowed me to interview their precious children. I salute you and your efforts to raise conscious, empowered children.

Thank you Mommy and Daddy for raising me to be a loving, strong, and passionate woman. Thank you to my six, Jashed, who always let me be myself and loved me unconditionally. You gave me the time to create and always shared the right words to keep me motivated. I love you to life. Let's keep this bucket list moving together. Khari, mommy loves you forever. Thank you for being willing to share me with the world. You are strong, wise, beautiful, and talented. Follow your dreams. Thank you to my family: "Heart Aunt" Sandy, Auntie Louise, my sister Tytannie, and Johnta. And thank you to the Jordan, Cousin, Tyler, Goodman, Barnes, Bogan, Davis, Fakhrid-Deen, and Crawford-Hutt families—we are all much thicker than blood. We made ourselves a family, didn't we? I have a strong network of friends who always have my back and I heartily thank them for the constant encouragement, feedback, and help with various stages of the manuscript—Mai Shiozaki, Ronda Brookins-Williams, Jason Smith, Monique Cook-Bey, Eleanor Seaton, Sean Long, Christal Mims-Williams, Christin Hill, Kim Cole, Erica Watson, and my lovely Delta Sigma Theta *sorors*.

To my incredible editor, Brooke Warner, thank you for believing in this manuscript and taking a chance on me. How we came together is truly serendipity. It was a pleasure working with you, and you have my full gratitude. Thank you to Krissa Lagos, Seana McInerney, and all of the individuals at Seal Press who have dedicated themselves to making this book an amazing reality. Thank you Debra Orenstein for making the contract process more manageable.

I want to wholeheartedly thank COLAGE for supporting me and believing in me and this work. We are family. Meredith Fenton, without you, this book would not be in the universe or the great hands in which it has been placed. I gave the baby to you, and you nurtured it and found it a loving home. Thank you for your friendship, guidance, research assistance, ability to help me find loads of interviewees, your emotional support, spot-on insights, and editing/writing support. You are a Goddess. Beautiful Beth Teper, thank you for allowing me to be part of the COLAGE world in a significant, unconditional, and loving way. Monica Canfield-Lenfest, thank you for your insights into the transgender community and for being there when I needed you. I also want to thank all of the staff, volunteers, and COLAGErs (past, present and future) that have contributed to this work, rooted for me, and placed this book where it needs to be.

Without my fabulous COLAGE Chicago families, there could be no me. Thank you for allowing me into your lives and hearts. I love you. From our union, we birthed this book. COLAGE Chicago rocks!

Shout outs to my fellow COLAGE crew, queerspawn, and special people who helped along the way. Jamie Larson, you are the one—always. Kisses and hugs to Vicki Larson, Jude Koski, Orson Morrison, Linda Howe, Chelsia

Rice, Bethany Lockhart, Tiffany Ross, Bonnie Fenton, and Ryan LaLonde (for your sunshine and diligent research on famous queerspawn). I also want to thank Abigail Garner for her friendship, support, long conversations, and for writing *Families Like Mine*.

Much gratitude and respect to my mentors, writing coaches, and critical supports. Robyn Schwartz, you are amazing and you gave this book so much when it was needed most. Thanks for getting this ship to the shore, and thank you for all of the editorial guidance and questions you provided to help me sort through my thoughts. I salute and adore you. I also want to thank my brilliant mentors and teachers who have given me roots and wings—Nnedi Okorafor, Esther Hershenhorn, Sandra Jackson-Opoku, Dr. Kelly Ellis, Dr. Brenda Aghahowa, Dr. Haki Madhubuti, and Bonnie Rubin.

A sincere thank you to anyone that I have forgotten to name that has assisted me in this long, arduous process. Charge it to my head and not my heart.

Thank you to all of the organizations, families, congregations, bookstores, and individuals who will tirelessly get this book into the hands and hearts of those who need it. A million thanks for your efforts and continued support.

—Love & Light, Tina

About the Author

Tina Fakhrid-Deen is a high school teacher, consultant, freelance writer, and community activist. For eight years, she was the volunteer coordinator of the Chicago COLAGE chapter that she founded in 2000. Tina provided resources to LGBTQ-headed families through monthly gatherings, constant phone/on-line support, book and media resources, and frequent presentations. She has presented on behalf of children living in LGBTQ families for organizations such as PFLAG, LadyFest, the Adler School of Psychology, Family Week, COLAGE, Family Pride Coalition, Rush Presbyterian—St. Luke's Medical Center, and Mountain Meadow Tina has been honored as one of the *Windy City Times* Top 30 Under 30 LGBTQ activists, profiled in the National Gay and Lesbian Taskforce's Family Policy Manual, and featured on the cover of the *Chicago Tribune* in an article about individuals growing up with LGBTQ parents. Tina holds a master's degree in Creative Writing and Black Literature from Chicago State University. She resides in Chicago with her husband and seven-year-old daughter.

ABOUT COLAGE

COLAGE is a national movement of children, youth, and adults with one or more lesbian, gay, bisexual, transgender and/or queer (LGBTQ) parent/s. COLAGE build community and work toward social justice through youth empowerment, leadership development, education, and advocacy. Visit our website at www.colage.org.

NOTES

SELECTED TITLES FROM SEAL PRESS

For more than thirty years, Seal Press has published groundbreaking books. By women. For women.

Listen Up: Voices from the Next Feminist Generation, edited by Barbara Findlen. $16.95, 978-1-58005-054-8. A collection of essays featuring the voices of today's young feminists on racism, sexuality, identity, AIDS, revolution, abortion, and much more.

Gringa: A Contradictory Girlhood, by Melissa Hart. $16.95, 978-1-58005-294-8. This coming-of-age memoir offers a touching, reflective look at one girl's struggle with the dichotomies of class, culture, and sexuality.

Laid: Young People's Experiences with Sex in an Easy-Access Culture, edited by Shannon T. Boodram. $15.95, 978-1-58005-295-5. This hard-hitting anthology paints a candid portrait of what sex is like—the good and the bad—for today's young people.

Get Opinionated: A Progressive's Guide to Finding Your Voice (and Taking A Little Action), by Amanda Marcotte. $15.95, 978-1-58005-302-0. Hilarious, bold, and very opinionated, this book helps young women get a handle on the issues they care about—and provides suggestions for the small steps they can take towards change.

Girls' Studies: Seal Studies, by Elline Lipkin. $14.95, 978-1-58005-248-1. A look at the socialization of girls in today's society and the media's influence on gender norms, expectations, and body image.

The Chelsea Whistle: A Memoir, by Michelle Tea. $15.95, 978-1-58005-239-9. In this gritty, confessional memoir, Michelle Tea takes the reader back to the city of her childhood: Chelsea, Massachusetts—Boston's ugly, scrappy little sister and a place where time and hope are spent on things not getting any worse.

Find Seal Press Online
www.SealPress.com
www.Facebook.com/SealPress
Twitter: @SealPress